What
We
Owe
Children

What
We
Owe
Children

The
Subordination
Of
Teaching
To
Learning

CALEB GATTEGNO

OUTERBRIDGE & DIENSTFREY
New York
DISTRIBUTED BY E.P. DUTTON & COMPANY

Library of Congress number 72-106612
First published in the United States of America
in 1970

Design: Samuel N. Antupit

Second Printing, February 1971

Outerbridge & Dienstfrey
200 West 72 Street New York 10023

Contents

Preface

This volume is the first to present as a whole an approach to teaching called "the subordination of teaching to learning." The discussion is oriented most directly toward two groups: educators in schools or school districts at the elementary and secondary levels and those in teachers colleges, both students and professors. But since parents also are educators, they too may find some use in the ideas examined in this text.

The approach was first developed and presented ten years ago for all educators concerned with teaching mathematics. Soon after it was extended to the tasks of those concerned with teaching reading, and in 1963 to teachers of foreign languages. In a number of seminars and workshops it has been extended to the fields of science, social science, literary studies, art, music, and physical education. In all areas, it led to an acceleration of learning and a greater yield in schools. The people who have used it know it is the only way of teaching that makes sense, and soon from new converts have come committed expounders. Such allegiance explains how this approach to education, without any official backing from anyone in a position of authority, has reached so many teachers all over the world.

In the United States it has proved itself as the one approach to education that can create hope where despair was the rule. It has fired with enthusiasm those who looked at "inner city" educational problems and were dismayed.

A radical transformation occurs in the classroom when one knows how to subordinate teaching to learning. It enables us to expect very unusual results from the students—for example, that *all* students will perform very well, very early and on a much wider area than before.

There are no gimmicks in this approach. Only the intelligent use of the powers of the mind in all the individuals involved, both teachers and students. But it is so different from what has been going on for so long that it requires a true conversion from the educator, so that he no longer neglects to consider the most important component of education, the learner himself.

The consequence of including the learner—which means that the classroom process of learning becomes one of self-education, the only real kind—is that teaching techniques and materials must be recast. The techniques are human throughout, the materials as varied as required. No magic wand exists that will change traditional teachers into teachers capable of using the new techniques: only serious study and serious trials in the classroom.

Another consequence is that national

standardized tests not only lose all power to inform the public on the achievement of students when they are taught in this manner, but the tests lose their meaning as such. They have always in any case reflected what *educators* were doing in schools and how well they were performing the task of instruction. The weaknesses of instruction were then placed on the shoulders of the students, and they were the only ones to fail.

Looking for objectivity, the standardized tests displayed only prejudice, the result of the teachers and investigators looking from outside and missing the dynamics of the mind.

Today we have the means to criticize tests seriously and to replace them with activities that truly reflect what learners do with themselves and also give teachers meaningful information on how to steer courses and develop realistic curricula. The need for knowing what one is doing exists all the time and only a cybernetic approach to the process of learning with continuous control via conscious criteria can be satisfactory to teachers, students, and public alike.

The role of the teacher will then be elevated to that of a scientist, thus permitting teachers to form a responsible profession and to deliver to each generation what it needs in order to meet its future.

1.

The Powers
of Children

Most of the things that are without importance to educators today, are the source of what is going to make us do a much better job in education.

What is the task of education? Is it not to provide students with the means to meet the future?

There is one thing that we all agree about with respect to the future, and this is that it is unknown—unknown absolutely if we project it far enough and relatively if we consider the relationship of tomorrow to yesterday, which seem not so different.

In devising a system of education, man may wish to stress what remains constant after the passage of time, but he can equally well stress that our world is becoming more and more "man-made" as against "natural," and that in such a world we would be on very shaky ground if we identified what will be with what is. The only way to be properly prepared and secure in a changing world is if we accept the future as unknown. (But really the world is always changing.) Such a view is all the more persuasive when we see that it leads to suggestions for doing the job of education that are at least as good as those that follow if we separate the remote and near future and treat them differently. That we must prepare for the unknown is my approach to education—and in a sense is everyone's approach.

Teachers in traditional schools—the schools we have today—know that what they know and have to teach is unknown to the learners. And they believe that they are making the unknown known by imparting their knowledge to their students. But has this belief proved right? How many readers of this book, for example, understand everything their teachers taught them? Or sixty or forty percent? And to what extent has the sixty or forty percent enabled them to meet what is new and strange? The answers are self-evident. Unfortunately, the traditional approach has not worked well. On the other hand, a method of educating for the future does exist—if we know how to acknowledge what is given us and already is in us, and with this, encounter what is but is not yet part of us.

It happened that every one of us as a child did precisely this. For a while we did not talk, we did not speak, and after a while we did both. That is to say, we met what was and we managed to make it our own. So every one of us as a child was really facing the unknown, meeting the unknown, and developing the techniques for doing it. But when we went to school, we found another technique in use: someone told us what was supposed to be known by us. Teachers told us, "You should know it," and the reason was, "Because I told you"— arrived at by putting together two ideas that are entirely unrelated: the pronouncement by the teacher and the retention or understanding by the student.

Two roughly drawn diagrams will assist us in comparing the way of working that is from the teacher to the student—the traditional method of schooling—and the way of working that is from the student to the world—the method of subordinating teaching to learning. The first diagram portrays the standard way of teaching.

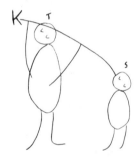

In this approach, knowledge is conceived as pre-existing and as coming down, through the teacher, from those gifted people who managed to produce it. (Let us note that in this country the phrase "knowledge industry" expresses just such a view of knowledge.) It is stored in special places called libraries which have books and more modern forms of containers. People who want knowledge have to go there and pick it up, in much the same way that they would acquire any other manufactured product.

Teachers are those people who take knowledge down from the shelves where it is displayed and hand it out to students who presumably need only memory in order to receive it. This process is conceived as the way the student comes to own knowledge. The key to this view—and to the whole traditional way of teaching—is the tacit belief that memory is a power of the mind.

Obviously it is. But still, memory can be strong or weak. La Rochefoucauld said around 1660 in a very short statement: "Man gladly complains of his memory, but not of his intelligence." Was he correct in his implication that memory is in fact a weak power of the mind?

To see that it is we need go no farther than to look at what is done by teachers in order to insure that their students retain the knowledge handed down to them.

Teachers give a *lesson*, thinking that they are passing knowledge on to their students, but since they do not actually know whether they have succeeded, they proceed to give the students *exercises*.

Why do they give exercise? So that what they themselves cannot do, the exercises will do: get the knowledge securely into their students.

But exercises usually are not sufficient, so teachers also give *homework*. What does homework do? What a teacher cannot do. If the teacher could finish the job in school during school hours, there would not be any need for any homework. That is why students get homework.

It does not end there either. There are also *reviews*. On Monday morning the class reviews what was done the week before. In January the class reviews what was done last term. And next year what was done the previous year. Teachers not only review and review, they also *test* whether students still hold the knowledge. And they do not

4

stop with one cycle of reviewing and testing. Reviewing and testing goes on for years because teachers know that many of their students do not retain the knowledge they are presented with.

So there is this accumulation of props, all to sustain the poor weak memory.

But nobody says that exercises, homework, reviewing, testing, then more exercises, more homework, more reviewing, more testing, and on and on, are there because memory is weak. We do not say that the whole traditional education is based on something that is weak, and that therefore the basis of education should not be memory. Yet the education offered in traditional schools—at least when we are concerned with transmission of knowledge — is described with precision by the above remarks.

This we call the subordination of learning to teaching, illustrated in the first diagram. I hope no reader believes I am trying to ridicule the situation with this diagram. For me, it is an exact illustration. The teacher with one hand gets some knowledge and with the other hand gives it out: that is the operation.

An advantage of such a teaching procedure is that it can be explained at the college level. Professors can explain to teachers how to present a subject and how to refine a presentation. Indeed, in their explanations they use the same approach they are passing on. The diagram applies equally to the work done at institutions of higher learning.

To understand that there once was good reason for Man to choose memory as the channel of instruction in spite of its inadequacies we need only to look back and place ourselves at a time when ways of recording events had not yet been invented. In our individual experience, then and now, we find that much of what we know how to do—talk, walk, breath while eating, etc.—expresses itself in automatic unconscious functionings often difficult to objectify and thus inaccessible to other people. On the other hand, the content of tales, legends, stories, gossip, etc., if repeatedly told, gains an existence of its own which we can attempt to preserve per se as we do objects. When recording of events was not available, the quality of the mind socially most valued was faithfulness (fidelity in the modern electronic sense), and verbatim retention became the highest attribute of a good mind. Since as children we show retention best after we have learned to talk, verbal retention understandably became the object of the care of teachers whether at home, in the forum, or at school. Tests in such a social setting were tests of retention for those who carried the tribal traditions.

When recording appeared, the attribute of retention could be weaker per se since it was supported by the record, and in fact it soon became second best to the record. But this change did not make societies discard the use of memory as the basis for teaching. There still was a stress on traditional transmission; no more individually oriented method of transmission had yet become acceptable to the Establishment. A stable society uninterested in questioning tradition was served well by transmission of well-preserved statements about wisdom and truth.

But in a changing world one discovers that the ability to forget is needed as much as the capacity to retain and that there is no value in taking the time to fix in one's mind what no longer obtains.

No one in such a world is prepared to pay a heavy price for what is no longer functional. This is the situation today. The success, such as it is, of the present system of education through memory results in fact from our own spontaneous use of ourselves as we go beyond the epistemology that describes our growth as greater and greater retention and shift ourselves to other ways of knowing.

Now, what is the alternative to the use of memory?

The alternative is to build on strength. And strengths exist. These I call the *functionings of children,* and they are the basis of all individual education, and now can be made the basis of institutional education.

What are the functionings of children? They could all become known to us because we all have been children. We have used these functionings, we have them in us, and we did with each such a good job, mastering it so successfully, that we do not have to do it again (except in an extreme situation, as with an accident that takes, say, half of one's brain, after which one has to learn to use the other half for the functionings involved with the missing half). On the whole, for example, we learned so well to sit that we do not have to learn to do it ever again. Sitting is one of the functionings of children.

When I was in my crib I worked tremendously hard. I knew that if (while lying on my back) I lifted my legs—which were quite easy to lift—with muscles reachable by my will, I was helping myself to learn to sit. Nobody showed me how to sit. Was any reader of this book taught to sit? Each person looked toward himself and saw for himself the problem of being on one's back and of learning to sit. One cannot say that sitting is instinctual. It takes months to learn. A man is not a little goat who is born having already practiced lots of things and an hour after its birth is standing on its feet. At six months I had not sat before. My mother did. I did not. I had to learn how to sit, and this I did for myself, as every reader did it for himself, in the crib.

If a child's accomplishments in his crib are not impressive, then nothing is impressive. There is no end to the (extraordinary) functionings we all accomplished as children. One of the most impressive is learning to speak. In my crib I discovered that if I worked on the muscle tone of my lips, that would permit me to gain entry into the field of the sounds of speech. I knew that I had to act on the muscle tone first, and by the sixth or seventh or ninth week of my life, I had learned the ways of doing this. And as I produced these ways I used my lips straightaway to produce new sounds, which in turn made me aware of other ways and so on.

As a child, nobody reading this book ever heard a word. In fact nobody ever heard a word. Ears hear voices. And voices are all different. We hear voices, and they differ in pitch and in stresses. There are all sorts of variations: one can have a deep voice or a smooth voice, a very quick speech or slow speech, and so on. And out of all these voices that represent the reality of the environment, each of us has picked up that component that we learned to call word. Every one of us has recognized words as being something one can add to the functioning of the throat one owns so that a sound comes out in a particular guise and is recognized by others as having been produced by one's voice. Children do not learn by imitation, otherwise they would speak at different pitches to the various people they come in contact with. That they do not is one reason that makes us say that children learn to make words through the use of their own mental powers—and learn to do it so well that for their whole life thereafter (barring an unusual accident) they continue to make words without any conscious preparation. (There are other reasons: how can a child even *see* the tongue movements that, if he learned speech through imitation, he necessarily would have to duplicate in order to talk?)

What do we learn about the mental powers of children from the fact that the ability to make words becomes one of their functionings? We learn first of all that children are equipped—we are all equipped—with the power of *extraction*, which obviously is very competent since it can find what is common among so large a range of variations.

Second, we have to acknowledge that children have the power to make *transformations*, for to learn to speak is to use transformations constantly. In every verbal situation in which someone is trying to tell us something, the words are to be used by us as they are by the others. The words cannot simply be repeated.

If someone says to me, "*This* is *my* pen," and I repeated it, I would be wrong; and if we were children, we might quarrel. Then perhaps I would see that I have to say something else to be at peace with the other person, and I might learn very quickly. In any case, I eventually will learn to say, "*That* is *your* pen."

Again, if I look at one person, a woman, and I

talk to her, I will use the word "you." But if I look at her and talk of a third person, a man, I must say, "he." Such transformations go on all the time. Indeed, there would be no pronouns in a language if there were no such thing as transformation.

So this is a second power used by children in the process of speaking and developed by it.

Further, everyone who has learned to speak has demonstrated an enormous competence in handling *abstractions*, for no particular word has an exclusive meaning of its own.

Words are signs, arbitrary signs, since each object, for example, can have as many names as there are languages. Not only do children have to extract words from the full packages represented by the voices they hear, they must also attach meaning to the words. Meaning must precede the grasp of what is used by the environment to refer to it.

Nouns, for example, cover classes of objects (*car* applies to all cars, *glass* to all glasses, whatever the make, shape, color, etc.). Verbs cover multitudes of actions or states (*jump* applies to a continuum of distances from the ground, *cry* to any cause for this kind of behavior). Adjectives cover spectra of impressions (*red, rectangular,* etc.) and so on. Children must learn to make the proper abstractions so as to give to words their particular agreed upon meaning, and they do learn.

No one can retain a noun without making allowance for all the changes in lighting, distance, angle of vision, etc., which constantly accompany our constant displacements in the environment.

So to talk I have to learn that I have to demonstrate that I can pick up—extract—something that is as subtle as words. I must

10

recognize the word within the voice that is used. I must also recognize what transformation is required in going from one situation to another. And I must learn, which I do through my powers of abstraction, the meanings attached to words. Therefore I have a functioning as a speaker at the age of two, that could give me a doctorate, for no doctoral student in a university has ever done as good a job equivalent to what we all did when we were one and two years of age, finding by ourselves how to acquire the extremely complicated system called language (which in English is more complicated than in many other languages).

Indeed because we all did it, it does not impress us very much. And in my career, in my work with developing new solutions to the problems of education, I have often been considered a fool for having been impressed. But when we look at children as owning the powers they actually have and at how they function, we are overwhelmed with the possibility for education. We are not discouraged, as we are when we look at memory as the only basis for progress.

There is one universal functioning without which nothing is noticed. This is the *stressing* and *ignoring* process.

Without stressing and ignoring, we can not see anything. We could not operate at all. And what is stressing and ignoring if not abstraction? We come with this power and use it all the time. I know that the pitch of my brother and the pitch of my father differ but I ignore the difference so as to comprehend that the words of one are comparable to the words of the other. I ignore that it is only the eye of my mother that I can see when she comes close to my cheek and kisses me. If I did not, the eye quite likely would frighten me. But I ignore this, and I stress the smell of the person. From this I know it is my mother. That is, I can shift my attention to another attribute that also belongs to her. If I did not do that I would not know that it was my mother that kissed me. To stress and ignore *is* the power of abstraction that we as children use all the time, spontaneously and not on demand, though in its future uses we may learn to call it forth by demand. And teachers insist that we *teach* abstraction to children through mathematics at the age of twelve!

What does it mean to possess a functioning, to know as children know how to eat, how to sit, how to speak?

What reader of this book literally remembers his native language? Not one. None of us remembers it, we function in it, we have at our disposal the "know-how" to do it. This is what it means to have a functioning.

The know-how leads to skill, the know-how is what we have within us that does not require conscious recall. It is just there. If I had to remember my speech, I would never be able to talk. Anyone observing himself will see that to have an intention to speak is sufficient for all of one's verbal elements to be available and for finding them adequate for one's intention. An individual need not call in these elements one by one; they come, the intention brings the appropriate words in and excludes the others.

Further—and here we move to another point and another power of children—when the words come out, it is the will that acts upon the speech organ for the words to be spoken in the way that the language expects them to sound.

Hence, there must be within us a control system that guides the making of these sounds.

We have established this system in our crib, the feedback mechanism that exists between our utterances and our hearing. All day long the vigilant ear attends to our speech. And what we developed as a result is reliable most of the time. An individual knows when he has made a mistake. He says: "Oh, that is not what I wanted to say." It is the ear that tells him this, not the throat. This task of organization and coordination does not exist when we are first born, we discover it in our crib, and we use it, practice it, refine it, and make it more powerful until it becomes an instrument for knowledge—knowledge that is meaningful within the criteria we have.

Now, as soon as we shift from acquiring facts through memory to acquiring them through functionings, we unify our experience in the duration of one life—for we always build on and integrate with what already exists and do not simply pile one fragment of information upon another—and we recognize that inner meaning is more important than outside authority. Meaning for our psychosomatic organism exists if it either falls readily within the sense of truth already at work or can be integrated in an enlarged functioning of the sense of truth. But in either case it is the person doing to himself what is required in order to receive the new. Hence the person is judging whether there is a reality (within him or outside) that agrees with the existing functionings or requires the widening of oneself to integrate the new. This adaptation of the self to the world is proof both of the malleability of the self and, more directly to the point in this context, of the

13

existence of inner conscious criteria capable of ordering either immediate integration or immediate change in order to achieve integration.

Such inner criteria, which all children have, are the epistemological consequence of the shift from an outside vision of man to one aware of individuals functioning for themselves in their world.

An approach to education that rests on the powers of children—the approach that I call the subordination of teaching to learning—can be illustrated in the following way.

Its contrast to the diagram illustrating the traditional approach is obvious.

Despite all that children know, in school we do not allow them to trust their own perception, only their teachers. At school, to the question "2 plus 3?" some children answer—"Five?" They do not answer "Five!" because they have not been allowed to use the basis of surety that exists in their perception. They have not been allowed to believe in their sense of truth. So knowledge becomes something that is passed on to them. Not something they own. This is the consequence of teaching through memory and not by functionings, and it brings us to the one last power developed in

14

the functionings of children that we need to examine for our present purposes.

The schools have a curriculum that is based upon the teachers providing children with showers of knowledge. Knowledge is so vast that, to make this approach manageable, we take a stretch of knowledge and divide it among thirteen or so years by separating it into little bits. And in its piecemeal quality, Chapter 1 of the first textbook resembles Chapter *n* of the last.

In the books for teaching a foreign language, for example, all the lessons have the same format. As if having learned something of the language does not change one. One always begins the same way and the lesson invariably follows the same pattern, ending in a test.

In this approach, there is no concern with one of the things that all of us know—that all of us go through—and that is, that practice gives one the capacity to undertake bigger tasks, to be involved in greater challenges. Is this not so? Is it not something that everybody knows, that practice provides us with the capacity to attack bigger tasks?

In my own case, I learned this as an adolescent when I lifted weights. Lifting weights teaches one a lot if one can learn more than lifting weights. I recognized that lifting weights made me have muscles that allowed me to lift bigger weights, and that when I lifted bigger weights, I got bigger muscles which allowed me to lift bigger weights.

But this is not the approach that we have imbedded in the curriculum. Instead we work in the same way throughout the entire curriculum and do not take into account that there is a law—*the law of the cumulative effect of learning*—

15

which can be described by saying once you have learned something, once you have mastered something, then you can attack a bigger task. The curriculum should be like a fan, opening up to more and more things, to bigger and bigger things.

These comments point the way to what we can learn from studying the functionings of children.

In the next two chapters we ask: How can these functionings be used in the process of education? We use as our examples first reading (at present a matter of great concern) and mathematics, and then a subject fundamentally different from these skills, social science.

2.

The Teaching of Reading and Mathematics

If I already know how to speak, what then is the problem of reading?

Writing is the codification of spoken speech, and reading its reverse process.

What is written is nothing if it is not speech. How do we bridge the gap between the two types of speech? This is the problem of teaching reading.

Everyone speaks. Spoken speech is a functioning, not knowledge, a functioning which involves listening, hearing, discriminating, production of sounds, control of the production of sounds, observance of the order of sounds, flow of words, and meaning.

Before anyone can reach spoken speech, he must already have access to meanings or he could retain nothing. No object has a name per se, and the name of an object means only something in the code (the language) that one has accepted. But an object, name aside, has a meaning of its own, and all of us have had the good sense from our crib and

later on, even without speech, to recognize
meaning, to gain access to meaning. And once we
have a general access to meaning, then we can put
different labels on it, and the labels will stick to
the meaning. Speech can come only after we have
grasped the existence of meanings. (We really start
with recognition of sound, of sequences of sounds,
and so on, before and while we go on to meanings.)
Once this has been grasped, then we soon reach a
proficiency that differs from grown-ups only in the
number of words we use and perhaps by the range
of interpretations we can add to them.

Because speech is arbitrary, because speech is
not necessary, we may change the place of our
living and use another speech. Speeches are not
necessary, but they exist. The fact that man has
produced speech may be called a human attribute,
but any particular speech or dialect is not in itself
necessary. What is common to all men is the
capacity to associate, to hold meaning, to hold
words through meanings, and to recognize how
words are being used by the people who use them
normally.

Given this, there is very little to do in order to
go from spoken speech to written speech. So little,
for example, that for Spanish-speaking people, it
takes only about six hours of practice to lead them
to mastery of their written code as used in
ordinary publications.

To go from spoken speech to written speech
entails no more than the acquisition of five
conventions. One of these is necessary. Spoken
speech being in time, for the jump to written
speech it was necessary to find the spatial system
that is isomorphic to time. The straight line
presented itself and was chosen. So, straight

lines—alignment—belong to all languages. But the other four conventions are not necessary. Writing is done:

    — vertically (from top to bottom) or horizontally (from the left or the right), one line following the other,

    — above or below the lines,

    — with space between the signs,

    — using some characters (Latin or Cyrillic . . .).

In English we start a sentence with a capital. That is not the case with Hindi or Arabic. *But all languages observe linearity because of time.* Each statement has a beginning and therefore we need to impose an orientation on the line. But the other conventions—vertical or horizontal, certain spacing between the words, a code (usually) of graphemes for phonemes (Chinese characters are exceptions), placement in regard to the line—offer alternatives.

So there are only these five conventions to master in order to learn to write and read. We go from one convention in speech to the corresponding one in the written form. This task is so simple that today one can say *that the problem of reading is solved.*

What is not solved is how to make teachers of reading, and analysts of reading difficulties, stop talking of irrelevancies, and make them look at the real issues.

Let us do what needs to be done.

To illustrate the subordination of teaching to learning in the case of reading, I shall refer to the approach that I have developed, known as *Words in Color.* The approach has been tested in many classrooms throughout the country (and elsewhere), and its success is proof that formal classroom learning can proceed on the basis of functionings and not memory.

Briefly put, the perspective behind this approach is the following:

— since learners already are speakers and already have used themselves adequately to conquer spoken speech, teachers of reading can start with all that this means in terms of their students' powers of the mind (many elements of which we outlined in Chapter One);

— since up to a point written speech is "isomorphic" to spoken speech—is another system in space of signs displaying what is found in the first system of signs (sounds) in time—we can put the stress on presenting the isomorphism and leaving the rest to the learners.

More specifically, if one accepts the proposition that such a set of characteristics as the five conventions listed above provide the framework for the transcription of temporal sounds into spatial signs, then we do not need to complicate things by demanding that the student learn to decode them within the language. If this can be learned with no reference to what is suggested by, say, English words (and it can), this should be our choice simply because it permits concentration, through games involving letters as signs without content, on the conventions—the basics—to be acquired. A child's mastery of spoken speech is evidence that he can handle—indeed, needs to do so if he is to learn effectively and efficiently—such "abstract" matters. Only after this point does the approach introduce games whose purpose is the mastery of the specific convention of a particular language. To learn these conventions takes very little time and once learned, will never be lost because the mastery is achieved by each child in terms of his own powers and his own inner criteria of truth, and because these conventions can immediately be employed in writing.

From then on it is a matter of using algebraic techniques to provide "word attack" through a recognition of how words result one from the other. There is much to be said about the relation between algebra and the powers of the mind. Here, it is enough to say that the child's mastery of the capacity to transform, according to the situation, "I" to "you" and so forth, shows that he is entirely capable of employing algebra as a tool for learning. Thus in reading, *substitution, addition, insertion,* and *reversals* generate thousands of words out of very few, the first few particularly chosen to exemplify the vowels or syllables that form spoken English speech.

Comprehension then follows from:

— the capacity to utter the signs seen, as words but with the flow of speech and the melody of the language,

— the capacity to attach the appropriate meanings to all the words uttered.

If in some cases meanings are lacking, then either the teacher uses a text to convey them (via the context) or has to forgo providing an understanding till the student reaches all the meanings called for by the context.

(Beyond these understandings of reading implied in the discussion, there are others rarely considered when one is concerned with the beginnings of the skill. Not all reading is for information. For instance, one may read for inspiration or edification. But all readings require correct decoding and the integrative schema formed of the rhythm and intonations of the spoken language.)

All of this is achieved in the classroom, without the aid of homework.

Let us now take the case of mathematics. How can the subordination of teaching to learning be utilized in the teaching of mathematics?

Every child meets in his language the names of numerals, and he can acquire these as he acquires other names. But this set of words is special: it is ordered. So children very soon learn these sounds, and as a result they then have at their disposal a frame of reference. A child can refer to this framework if he wants to answer the question, "How many of this or that are there?" But in order to say how many objects there are in a set, he needs to create and to observe another rule—that of the one-to-one correspondence. For to answer the question, he must have observed that:

— there are two sequences, one of physical gestures (made by the hand, the neck, the ocular muscles . . .) and one of noises,

— the two have to be synchronized, and

— he has to control them.

So any child who can answer correctly the question, "How many?", by giving the corresponding numeral has demonstrated that he can retain the sequence of noises, that he can make the two sequences observe the order in the one (sound) sequence, and that he can make the one-to-one correspondence. (This is discussed more fully in the Appendix.) So if one asks, "What is counting?", we can say: "It is the answer to the question, 'How many?' "

22

Having learned to make all the noises that signify numerals does not make a child into a user of numbers, only into a person who knows how to make noises in a certain order and how to observe certain rules of correspondence. When does one learn to count? At the age of two perhaps, when one has certainly demonstrated that one can do the above on a number of different sets.

Teachers of children will say that the greatest power of the mind is the capacity to transform. Anyone who speaks and speaks properly—as many two year olds can do very easily—can transform according to his perception of the situation and according to the criteria that he has mastered and understood.

We teach a child to learn to say, "2 apples plus 3 apples make 5 apples," "2 pens plus 3 pens make 5 pens." What has he proved to us in learning this? That he knows that 2, 3, and 5 are three operators that go together, that 2 and 3 can be passed from apples to pens to pears to chairs and so forth. This is an important accomplishment. But teachers say children have to know that 2 plus 3 is 5. What do they mean? They mean that 2 apples and 3 apples is concrete, that 2 pens and 3 pens is also concrete, and that such a concreteness does not give children a proper grasp of the abstract concept of 2 and 3 and 5 and of the relationship 2 plus 3. But is this so?

Nobody has ever been able to reach the concrete. The concrete is so "abstract" that nobody can reach it. We can only function because of abstraction. Abstraction makes life easy, makes it possible. Words, language have been created by man, so that it does not matter what any reader evokes in his mind when he sees the word red, so

23

long as when we are confronted with a situation, we shall agree that we are using the same word even if for different impressions. Language is conveniently vague so that the word car, for example, can cover all cars, not just one. So anyone who has learned to speak, demonstrates that he can use classes, concepts. *There are no words without concepts.* If the opposite were true, children would quarrel again and again. If John meets John, either would say, "Don't call yourself John. I am John, not you." A child would meet someone and say, "Don't say 'I', I alone can say 'I.' " Obviously children's behavior in this and other instances is telling us that they manipulate classes mentally, that they manipulate transformations and classes, and that they know how to become more and more precise in looking for the intersection of different classes.

Therefore, how can we deny that children are already the masters of abstraction, specifically the algebra of classes, as soon as they use concepts, as soon as they use language, and that they of course bring this mastery and the algebra of classes with them when they come to school.

Most of us cannot conceive that this is so. We want to teach the algebra of classes at the college level, so we cannot say that children own it at the age of two. Why do we believe we have to wait until they are in college to teach them all this? Because, historically speaking, a grown man, Mr. X., discovered the algebra of classes and then wrote a paper on it and impressed the world of adults in, say, 1874. So we can not teach it before college.

The essential point is this: algebra is an attribute, a fundamental power, of the mind. Not of mathematics only.

Without algebra we would be dead, or if we have survived so far, it is partly thanks to algebra—to our understanding of classes, transformations, and the rest. I have noted the place of algebra in the process of teaching reading. This was not just an arbitrary technique. Since reading is a function of the mind, everyone must use algebra in order to read.

On this cornerstone enormous structures can swiftly be built.

The two statements "2 apples plus 3 apples makes 5 apples" and "2 pens plus 3 pens makes 5 pens," when mastered by a student, tell us that he knows how to put operators together. That is what the statements would say to teachers. What the student has done is to shift from apples to pens. Would not such a shift form a route immediately for: 200 plus 300?

What is the difference between the noise "apple" and the noise "hundred?" Can we not apply the operators to both noises? "Hundred" can be considered a noise like "apple." Is it not so? Likewise "billion?" So whole areas become immediately accessible to the young student if we understand that he brings with him the algebra of classes and if we subordinate our teaching to the already demonstrated capacity to learn.

Another attribute a child brings with him is the ability to notice differences and assimilate similarities. What does this mean? Aristotle put the ability to perform this operation at the foundation of basic logic and every child owns it: he brings it with him. Every child knows that the basis of living is to recognize differences and similarities.

Of two cups of the same make, we can hold one cup with the handle in front, the other so that the

25

handle is at the back. One may be pink, the other white. We still say both are cups, not two distinct kinds of objects, a pink object without a handle, a white object with a handle—but cups and that there are two of them.

We would say otherwise if we could not ignore differences and find the attributes that bring them together, as well as see the attributes that separate them. To separate them I say: one is pink and one is white. Do I need more than perception to put them together and separate them? All children have done this again and again. They recognize that a sound they have produced is very much like a sound produced afterwards, although it is in their memory, and differing a lot from the sound they are producing now. It is in their flesh, they know it. This, too, is part of mathematics, and one more element of the structure on which we can build in teaching mathematics.

Another power of the mind we use in subordinating teaching to learning in mathematics is the power of *imagery*.

Every one of us knows of the fantastic things that can happen in our dreams and nightmares. Looking both at the dynamics of imagery and at how it affects the content of our dreams, we can learn a great deal about what children bring with them to their mathematics studies.

The type of transformation met in this context, when the teacher calls upon mental evocations to advance mathematical understanding, is one that remains in contact with mental energy, keeps some continuity between the initial and the final forms of the images (which are dynamic, as in dreams), and produces effects that display the algebras applied to them. When concentrating on imagery,

one is more aware of content than of
transformation and stresses images per se all
through the process.

By asking students to shut their eyes and to
respond with mental images to verbal statements
enunciated by the teacher, one makes them aware:

— that in their mind imagery is connected
with the rest of their experience, and

— that in itself it is a power.

Indeed this type of relationship between teacher
and students can be used to generate whole
chapters of mathematics. The key here is the
dynamic attribute of imagery, which can be seen as
being equivalent to certain mathematical
properties.

For example, a teacher can verbally describe
that when two drops of water strike at the same
time the surface of a bucket full of water, they
generate ripples which one can look at as two
families of concentric circles. Then together, the
teacher and the students can explore through
imagery alone the mathematical properties of these
moving circles. By singling out some circles of one
family and relating them to one circle of the other
family, one obtains a classification of pairs of
circles in the same plane. By pairing them up, one
can obtain as loci of the intersections conics (and
their degenerate cases) and so on. These discoveries
the students make from examining the content of
their vision. (It is also possible to do all the work
visually and silently, using animated drawings on
films.)

Because images are dependent on our will, once
we begin deliberately to employ them, we can very
soon obtain an awareness that indeed imagery is a

power of the mind, and it can yield in a short time vast amounts of insights into fields that become almost sterile when the dynamics are removed from them.*

Algebra is present in all mathematics because it is an attribute of the functioning mind. Imagery is present at will and can remain present while the mind is at work on it or on some element within it.

Who can doubt that many more children will be at home with mathematics when features of it are presented to them as the recognition of what one can contemplate within one's mind when it is responding to mental stimuli.

These comments show the vast potentialities that lie before education when teaching is subordinated to learning.

I must add one more point about reading and mathematics. Both of these studies are what I call *know-hows*. There is another type of study, which I call *understandings*. A serious failure of the traditional school is that it does not recognize this distinction.

The know-hows require a very different technique from understandings. Know-how requires concentration, requires that we cut ourselves off from distractions and be exclusively with the point to be mastered. Imagine learning to drive a car and being needled by someone all the time. What will happen? Or try to make a long addition while someone talks to you interestingly.

---

*Many of the educational purposes obtained by animated films can be achieved by a simple instrument called a geoboard, on which rubber bands provide the dynamics. Since children can generate structurations with the rubber bands upon the very scant structures designed on the geoboards, the manipulations of this instrument blend action with perception and perception with action, so that the users are forced to note dynamics as well as images.

Know-hows require a "schizophrenic" attitude. Understandings require the opposite—that we make ourself vulnerable, that we are touched. And at school, we treat all subjects in one way.

Today this distinction can make a difference, a big difference. Social sciences study relationships between people. We have to know others, we have to open to them—not to remember that so and so was born on such a date. Know-how is not knowledge, it is a power. Understanding is another power. The fact that we can function and can recognize and can say that something has made an impact on us is the proof that we are going to be acquainted with knowledge which is part of us, that we now own knowledge and are not simply carrying around pieces of it like individual bundles on our backs.

In the next chapter, we turn to social science and how it can be approached through the subordination of teaching to learning.

3. The Teaching of Social Science

In the last chapter, our discussion, for obvious reasons, had the greatest application to the earliest school grades. Here the discussion widens to include higher grades—say, through high school— and older students.

No one will dispute that social sciences have been included in the curriculum because we believe that they have a role to play in the education of the young generation, that they can help make the young generation aware of some components of social living and better prepare them for the tasks ahead.

One can become conscious that a reality called society with its dynamics exists either through a clash with it or accidentally, by finding in one's readings, for example, that certain civilations never had some of the institutions we are used to. There are other ways but these two are important here and prepare the ground for the pedagogical section that follows.

Man first studies the means within himself that allow entry into the environment. He goes on to ask questions about his own involvement in the environment only when this relationship breaks down. Such questioning leads him to reach to the core of his self, his own consciousness. Today another type of breakdown is forcing men to take harder looks at what they did in their latest involvements with the environments—those of man with man. The pressure from the breakdown is generating both criticism of the past and a desire to enter the future with fewer chances of making comparable errors. Though there is no guarantee that greater mistakes will not be made, there is a possibility that we will make them less often if we are serious in our will to know better how to harmonize the social forces unleashed in every section of our societies. To harmonize them does not mean to yield to them, or to drift among them in any direction, or to offset their momentum with patchwork repairs, but to *renew* ourselves so as truly to extend our awareness till all the human landscape is in our inner social vision as easily as our earth is encompassed by the eye of astronauts a few thousand miles from it.

To obtain this for all men is obviously the purpose of social studies.

The majority of today's adults believe that because they are aware of social intercourse everyone should be. Still, only a few years earlier they themselves were living in a state that did not require this awareness. Such a change has important implications for the study of social science, and we need to be quite clear that in the process of our growth, life demands of us that we master a succession of separate realms (each of them vital for the individual) before we concentrate on the succeeding ones.

The preceding discussion has already touched upon some features of this development. For example, we saw that we are nonspeakers for months because we must first master the functionings of our senses so that we can, among other things, find an entry into the speech of our environment. We saw that to master our senses we must learn to use criteria that are connected with the realm of sound to be able to instruct our vocal organs to attempt what our ears have received and our minds have sorted out and assimilated. Our mouth spoke and our ears heard, and between the two arose a man-made correspondence that may have somatic components but is definitely mental.

Here we take the analysis further.

We become adolescents only when we have secured the world of action and played enough of the games that enable us to master the demands of relating to our natural environment. Only then can we afford the time to investigate the realm of feelings and throw ourselves into the study of such concrete relationships as friendship, love between the sexes, and love of humanity or of our group. How else can man grow—does man grow—than by involving himself in the possible expressions of himself? The passion displayed by adolescents, their resistance to any interference, are only signs of the importance that this study of relationships had been to each of us in our own flesh. It is no more or less intense than every one of the involvements that preceded it—for example, the involvement in games of action, or in dreams of action—but it is more visible and perhaps demands more time to be completed and may leave traces in future life that are more easily recognizable than those of the earlier involvements.

As adolescents we do not really understand what it is to make money, apart from asking for what we need or taking it. The adolescent perspective is one of instant fulfillment rather than one of dedication to an enterprise that may leave some profit.

We can take as self-evident that the experiences of adolescents, because they involve others and may also involve procreation, are vital to the awareness of the realm of social experience.

Now, once we have seen that in our own life we have been solicited differently by different realms for various durations and that we cannot reverse the orders of their appeals to enter each of them in turn, and having seen that among these realms social consciousness is a late comer in our own life, we then become fully aware of the coexistence of people involved in different realms but living under the same roof or in the same space, in school, street, city, state, country, and planet. What is this but one of the essential features of man that social science attempts to illuminate?

Today most people are troubled by the generation gap, a phenomenon that only underlines the fact that most of us are fully busy living what seems vital to us and are doing this without a sense of relativity and therefore without understanding the importance to each individual of what each is going through in his own life. Both parents and children know themselves as misunderstood, and both ask to be understood in their own terms. Much later, however, each of the sides finds that it had exaggerated its demands—for it no longer feels the stress of the earlier period.

The generation gap is one of the lights we can

use to be sure of the truth that life asks of us different functions at different periods of our life and that it is therefore wrong to use any one vision of any one period as if it were forever true.

These considerations lead us to a central notion: relativity is demanded by the reality of life. Only the perspective of relativity enables us to approach each individual without preconceptions and to uncover the true place of every one of us and the importance of what an individual is living through at any one moment of history.

Another aspect of the essential relativity of life is revealed by the fact that although the majority of adults today are socially minded and prove it by their capacity to form all the needed pressure groups to obtain recognition, adults have not always been like this in history, not even all of the adults forming any particular pressure group.

Indeed, the fact that adults have not always been socially minded is one of the reasons why social studies appeared on the scene at a certain date and why it has been possible to make a place for them in the school curriculum. In broad terms, what happened was that with the awareness of themselves as being socially minded, some men explored some aspects of their individual consciousness and found in it the elements that form the notions of the social sciences. When enough people did this—studied their awareness of society—the sciences were established with claims to positions in universities, funds for research, societies to promote the findings, journals to propagate the views of the leaders in these fields.

What does this mean? Because social studies have a date, I can say that they were not of interest to most individuals, not even to a few of them, before that date. And because the study of anything means the preoccupation of men with some aspect of their own being, we must assume that before anyone became aware of this dimension of consciousness, of men in distinction from society, there was nothing to study in that direction. So we must recognize quite simply that some individuals are socially aware and some are not and that this difference is a difference of consciousness, the key to all studies. In considering now to present social studies in the schools, we must keep such differences clearly in mind.

For those students who bring their own spontaneous interest, there is no need to consider the problem of motivation, only the need to find the criteria by which to select what to study and how.

But with regard to those who are not yet socially sensitive, a number of important questions arise. How does one bring the transcendental, that which does not exist for them, within their reach? Or is it impossible to do this? Is it really worth anything to include social studies before an individual manifests an awareness of the existence of the dynamics of society. Or is it possible to find the forms that foreshadow social living or will be able to be transmuted into social experience with economy and efficiency when awareness becomes spontaneously social?

Anyone who knows anything of child development and human growth recognizes that over the range of one's schooling almost everybody passes through three stages of social awareness: in the first, he in fact has no such awareness; in the second, he is an apprentice of social living—he lives something he does not yet comprehend; in the

35

third, he is moving towards a mastery of social dynamics—he begins to comprehend his experience. We can legitimately conceive of these stages as mapping out the direction in which every man is set. Our task, then, is to offer techniques and materials that at each stage will adequately educate the awareness as it manifests itself.

There is no question here of any presentation of history or geography with economics, anthropology, and so forth added to "modernize" the curriculum, and of course nothing of the traditional requests of schools that students remember what they have met in textbooks, films, museums, etc. (which encounters may leave a random impact, or none at all, or even the opposite of what anyone would understand as social education).

But if there is no question of subject matter, as it is commonly understood, there is a question of techniques, because we wish to educate awareness: first, the awareness of what one would have been had one been born in other times and other places; second, the awareness of what men have done in order to live together and how they used this awareness to fulfill themselves; third, the awareness of a man-made universe where mastery of the underlining dynamics leads to a "better" world for oneself and perhaps for all.

For students of the first stage, social living is part of natural living, and for their studies no discussion of either is contemplated, only reactions to such natural social living in terms of whether it helps the realization of one's self-chosen ends. At this stage, one aims at providing experiences that implicitly will convey a sense of what man has done with himself over the ages. Though some social relations and some social happenings are perceptible to the people in this group, the significance of such situations remains transcendental and no useful purpose can be served in having the group examine them more closely.

For the second group the movement of the members from natural social experience to a sense of participation in social life does not generally entail the acceptance of responsibility for more than oneself and a few selected others.

For the third group, the educational objective is to involve students in the direct experience of social dynamics. The educational objective here is to offer slices of life so that explicit experience can take place by proxy. Awareness of oneself as a participating member of a number of groups with different social functions would in time permit one's sensitivity, intelligence, and actions to provide oneself with a special place—say, as a leader of a group—in one or more societies. This experience could lead to manipulation of others, but it could also lead to a mastery of social dynamics that could make one into a successful negotiator, or a politician, or a civil servant, or an administrator, etc.

We will discuss the techniques and materials for presenting social studies to each group in turn.

I.   Rarely do our young children choose their environment. Their parents settle where they themselves want to live or must live. Moreover, one is born in a certain home as much as one is born in a hilly or flat region, without a choice for the composition of one's family, its standards of living, the language spoken, the rites observed, etc. All these circumstances appear to one's senses as if they were given, and they are not any more questioned by young children than is the fact that the sun rises in the east. Hence for most of us during our first years of life, the social environment can be considered as much imposed on us as the terrain and the climate. Children take in these characteristics and are also at peace with, say, much or little food or with much or little snow or winds.

Such acceptance represents the first level of social awareness.

At this stage, even when a child sees a site become a building, what strikes him first is that both the site and the building are part of the landscape. Similarly a slap from one's father is as much a pressure from the environment as is a wound from a fall.

Hence to provide social education at this level of awareness is to develop a sense of relativity between the various lives on earth at different times and places *in terms of what one takes for granted*—shelter, habits of dressing, feeding, moving from place to place, of defending oneself against attacks from others, etc.

Because it is awareness we want to reach, we have to offer to children, at this stage and later, those *aspects* of living by others that can make sense to them in a *manner* that makes sense to them. At the age of six, no one is really moved by how the ancient Egyptians found what belonged to whom when the flood waters receded. But one is ready to put on a garment resembling the garment seen on a bas-relief, particularly if one has helped make it.

It is not the history of Egypt or Greece we shall offer our students but rather the acquaintance with as many of the elements of the social environments of a number of peoples as can be brought to the classroom through the activities of the students. Teachers can much better focus the attention of their students on a succession of fields of study involving action than they can today through a verbal presentation of any of the times and places where history has been recorded.

So much of the "appearances" of social living can be made available to children without any question of value being asked, without imposing on them the unnecessary and at this stage useless effort at confronting the profound questions of why or of cultural influence. Yet, in our presentation, which develops awareness and does not supply lists of facts, we lay the groundwork for such questions.

The techniques of re-enacting actually or virtually the selected forms of social living can involve children in sessions in which they feed themselves; make and use household items as some peoples do; entertain themselves and guests; use different tools of different peoples; produce art works akin to those of various groups; speculate as to how events known to have happened ever could happen in view of what we know, say, of a people's technology.

More than a recognition of the relatitivity of human societies is to be gained by the students through such activities; the children also become aware of the range of their own and every individual's capabilities. Thus, because the normal questions asked by children at the first level of awareness are concerned with actions and perceptions, it is possible to involve the children in exercises that extend their capabilities beyond what is required normally by present-day living. For example, today no archery is demanded of us. But archery can be taken up as a study of what was demanded of our ancestors when they themselves were young. Likewise with many other skills that normally seem beyond us but are so only because they are not practiced.

Since some societies have perfected some of the possibilities of man to such a degree, it may be to our advantage as a human society to learn that through education and some practice we could each develop the somatic capabilities that would go to make us masters of the now absent and, to the child, unsuspected manners of a given civilization and culture.

In short, the purpose of social studies at this stage is not to provide knowledge (bookish and verbal) but to offer opportunities to be acquainted with oneself as one who, when it is a matter of using one's soma, is capable of acting as all men do or did.

But because we no longer need to be all through our adult life knights or pirates, we take only the time to be acquainted, mostly virtually, with what such lives demand of men in terms of resistance, agility, alertness, vigilance, etc.

This makes the social sciences educational at these stages if used in such a way.

II.   At the second level, building on the awareness that men produced varied forms of social living, forms that have been looked at in the first stage of social studies, it is now possible to enable students to enter into the lives of peoples so as to inquire more consciously into the beliefs, the norms, the trainings for the various demands of life which characterized these peoples.

To do this, we can begin by using the considerable artistic gift of writers like Homer, Virgil, Shakespeare, Cervantes, Tolstoy, etc., to recreate with minute details the inner atmosphere in the life of ordinary people. Or we might start with some of the extravagant historic films of Hollywood, which generate emotions more easily than do books, and from this beginning move on to check the veracity of scenes and feelings by comparing them with some of the written sources of these stories.

That fiction, legend, history exist is one of the lessons that can be learned from such comparisons. That history cannot be totally separated from belief, opinion, bias may be another. (The awareness that to be interested in history is a special bent that few peoples have cultivated, is a finding that pinpoints one of the fundamental sources of social sciences as such.) Through such materials, the awareness, for example, that self-interest, when it is narrowly cultivated, generates conflicts between individuals as well as peoples, can be almost indefinitely illustrated when looking at nations—other than one's own—that enter struggles reaching the level of wars. Looking at individual civilizations and the cultures each contains, it is also possible to convey to the students of this age both the general molding forces contained in every religion and the diversifying forces that reside in the physical environment.

In terms of awareness, we look at history as the process of making explicit, through successive generations, the human promises bequeathed by the founder or founders of given civilizations. So long as there is more to make explicit in their basic outlooks, civilizations go on. As soon as these basic outlooks stop inspiring, decadence can set in.*

It is an easy task to recast in terms of awareness what men have lived over the centuries, and it is not too difficult to offer this as a number of courses of study to occupy students for years—courses of study that are self-motivating precisely because of the involvement of the students' consciousness in the movements of other consciousnesses.

The inspirational value of a "Temple of Greatness" for growing minds has been noted by every perceptive teacher. Young men and women who are finding themselves can more easily be put in contact with their own dynamic self when they are put in contact with the expanded self of the great men of all civilizations. That we can live strong emotions in being involved, by proxy, in certain situations, proves the value of these situations for our growth and the educational impact they can have as they open our sensitivity towards lives that are not actually ours. In this way, dry facts are filled with life by the students and their generous self.

Thus, at this stage, the acquisition of knowledge is subordinated to the concern of finding oneself as a member of humanity as it stretches over the centuries and the corners of our planet. Our aim is to help our students gain the status of man and

─────────

*Similarly, the sciences of man (which include the natural sciences) reach impasses when scientists no longer renew themselves and acquire new insights. This is also true of the social sciences as well as of their application, which is the living out by groups of their common awarenesses.

recognize that besides natural forces and our own physical forces, other forces are known to man: love, ideas, ideals, identification, etc.

Acting, used in the first phase of social studies, is obviously one of the very ancient educational techniques employed by groups to educate themselves, and should be used in this phase also. Today as yesterday it remains important to achieve participation of this sort, as either actor or spectator or both.

III.   It is, however, much easier to re-enact history and to learn about the behaviors of "schematized" people than it is to make sense of the social life around one.

The third phase of social education can be offered half as a study of history recast in terms of social dynamics and half as a continuous effort to make sense of our contemporary environment.

The study of one's social environment has already been suggested by many social scientists as curriculum for this level. Adolescents who have developed in themselves both moral sophistication and social involvement can approach any one of the burning issues that concern adults. The television programs of every day raise questions that could become focal points for the classroom sessions called lessons. Teachers may themselves be activists or simply involved citizens and, if they forgo the desire to convert people to their views, can perhaps learn to be a focus for the study of prejudice, opinion making, bias, etc. A direct study of brainwashing can be available in the classroom.

Besides these studies of what goes on in the present environment (which leads to assessing articles, editorials, and essays in magazines, newspapers, reports, etc.), the study of history, geography, ecology, anthropology, ethnography, and various literatures is open for those who want to know:

— how one gathers evidence and evaluates it,

— where men's qualities and defects can lead them,

— which important insights are needed to make sense of life as a whole.

The materials for this period are so numerous that the ideal tools to put in the hands of these adolescents is a list of fruitful themes to explore.

Because of the conquests made by the social sciences over the last century or so, man in the West today has reduced much of the mystery to which we exposed our student in the second phase of providing a social education. Social engineering came of age and anyone can acquire its techniques through cool and determined study. Today high school students achieve easily what was so difficult to achieve by much older people three or four generations ago. They do not need transcendental notions to get involved in social actions. Social dynamics, like physical dynamics, has become neutral, and the knowledge of them is now available to all indiscriminately.

The point must be well understood. Science, by stressing that what one man knows can be known by all men, has put at everyone's disposal the workings of a diesel engine—and the workings of various social institutions. Institutions now have only the attributes of schemas, and they can be analyzed, changed, improved, like engines. If an adolescent can learn to take to pieces an engine and put it together by sheer observation, so, in effect, can he do the same with institutions once they gain the status of "things," which is precisely what has happened to institutions by virtue of the studies of social science.

The revolution among the young in regard to their desire to dismantle and rebuild the institutions around them—a revolution that took so many adults by surprise these past years—is merely a duplication of what happened in so many other fields: that anything that can be known can be dominated and used. When this occurred with mathematics or physics or technology, the older generation congratulated itself. When it occurred, more or less surreptitiously, on the social scene, adults, unaware that history was doing its job of sifting to younger ages the conquests of previous generations, found themselves unable to comprehend the event and have reacted to it at random, with bewilderment and sometimes anger.

The ample dialogue of the generations we are witnessing today is telling us that men no longer fear and worship society, that they see it, in the terminology used here, as one of the transcendentals of yesterday which today is instrumental and neutral.

But it can also tell those who wish to hear it that humanity has entered a new layer of existence where new transcendentals exist and operate as the inspiration that provides the optimism for tomorrow.

Once more the triple movement of awareness—from contact to analysis and mastery—can be witnessed in those who suspect the fullness of the future; who are experimenting with a world-wide democracy embracing every member of our humanity, a concept that is an extension of what social consciousness has given us who are forging ahead and speak in terms of the knowledge of neutral science, of man as obviously an inhabitant of the Earth.

4.

The Role of the Teacher

Even the most liberal educator, other than A. S. Neill himself, or someone working with very special problems in special education, finds it hard to conceive of schools as places where no knowledge will be acquired.

By knowledge we can all agree that we mean the accumulated collection and interpretation of data in any field that men have made theirs by study.

Does the concept Knowledge apply to such matters as: "living in peace with oneself"? or "learning to be a responsible person"? or "being faithful to one's sense of truth even if it leads to rebellion against the environment and one's rejection from it"?

Many will say no.

But can one be called a teacher who does not see that data, and not only interpretation are involved in these issues—data that may not be of the sort that can be duplicated but that are none the less perceptible, expressible, communicable, and perhaps understandable?

Of course "teacher" as with many other words (master, religion, and so forth, not to mention reading), has several meanings, and we should watch the shift from one to another in different contexts. Here it will mean a person who selected among many social openings the option of working with people in institutions so that these people learn to use their time to increase their experience and to acquire the means and criteria to interpret experience. This meaning may well include all teachers currently employed in schools anywhere, even if a number of them do much more than the above and a larger number do it but are unaware of doing it.

To most teachers working today, teaching is an adult function already well defined in the books—one that was used in their case (and not so badly after all, since they have learned enough to earn a living) and with contemporaries who are now moving or have moved towards becoming the ruling generation of their nation; one which they know is criticized by liberals and others, some of whom they call extremists, but which they believe has not been and cannot be replaced by a better approach; and one which is expounded by most professors of education who write the books that fill the library shelves and which therefore must have some basis in fact.

Indeed, teachers are justified in doing what has always been done, until they see why they should change and whom they are pleasing. Is it a critic, who perhaps cannot do his own job as well as they do theirs in the circumstances they face? Or a visionary reformer, who has identified with his

48

vision and so cannot find any flaws in it even though it may contain some? Or an enthusiastic inventor, who clearly has something to offer but offers it as a panacea?

Since teachers on the whole are employees of some school board and the terms of their employment does not usually demand any loyalty to any educational theory and practice, they are free to teach as they were taught, which is what most do, and free to innovate so long as they keep within certain general bounds, not specified in many instances until after they have been crossed. This situation has led to a feeling in many observers that educational reform in a "free" society is impossible, for when it is not the teachers who refuse it, their employers may well prevent them from accepting it, and in the latter instance teachers would then have to return to traditional methods and approaches (against their own choice) or seek a job somewhere else or open their own school, all difficult moves.

What is new today that may break such a deadlock and permit change to take place is partly contained in the previous chapters (in the discussion of powers other than memory to which to direct one's teaching efforts) and partly in the discussion that follows.

Teachers, like all people, agree to be wrong up to only a certain point. They would not be among those who, desiring to go to California, would travel, say, by horseback from New York City if they could afford to go by jet plane. Teachers, like all people, know the difference between a tedious effort and an easy one. And like all people, they prefer the easy one.

Teachers who can be shown that their self-interest dictates that they make some changes in their present classroom activities will endeavor to make them.

What might be the form of such a presentation? Certainly, it would include discussion at the rational level, assuming that the arguments could be translated from the verbal medium to imagery that met a teacher's affectivity directly.

But more essentially, it likely would include a demonstration in which the proposer of the change shows he can enter the teacher's situation and obtain—with changes available to the teacher—results distinctly better than those the teacher ordinarily obtains and believes to be the norm in such circumstances.

Demonstrations have entered the field of education as the device that teachers use to judge personally what is being offered them, in contrast to the use by academic people of research reports to argue the truthfulness of particular beliefs. Teaching is an applied field and against any proposal for improvement, the pragmatic criterion obtains. Ultimately even academic research on teaching resorts to the test of trial (although the reporting on it looks like an exercise in some other medium than classroom teaching).

Teachers may be impressed by academic research, but they are not influenced by it. They demand that ideas be translated into classroom action. This in turn can only be judged through one's own perception and interest, by the transferability of the approach to oneself, by its relevance as estimated by one's conceptions, values, and preconceptions. Teachers would not agree to take on new approaches that contradict their values and interests simply for the sake of someone else, even if their own approach can be seriously criticized precisely in terms of its values and the interests that shape it.

This legitimate—though in some senses unrealistic—attitude of teachers that any new approach satisfy their own self-interest, needs to be taken into consideration in any proposal if it is to find an audience among teachers.

In sum, teachers will agree to become an audience for a new proposal and agree to give it a chance if its proposer:

— attempts to formulate it in terms that take them into account,

— is capable of demonstrating to them in their own terms what he wants them to accept,

— meets in the demonstration a set of criteria that teachers apply to others (even if some of them do not permit the criteria to be applied to themselves) and which they consider as safeguards in performing their job,

— does distinctly better than themselves but in a way that is distinctly compatible with their temperament, ideals, ways of working.

Teachers *can* be a block to progress in education if the advocates of new proposals do not know how to bridge the gap between themselves and an audience that in fact comes to exist because teachers seek progress and are prepared to look at anything that promises improvement. But it is not the duty of teachers to convince themselves of the particular advantages of any given new approach, since they are practitioners and can keep their job so long as they teach as they have been taught. Thus, it becomes the duty of authors of proposals for change to ensure in their proposals all that is needed to make the change a possibility. This is the task before them.

Further, the more a particular change demands from teachers, the more the proposer must work on details and provide special demonstrations to clarify the ways this change can occur.

Subordination of teaching to learning demands a great deal, but it also gives back a lot in return. Now that this approach has been demonstrated all over the world and for teaching areas including basic subjects (mathematics, reading, writing, spelling) science, physical education, and foreign languages, it has begun by itself, so to speak, to acquire an audience—mainly among practicing teachers. As a result, now that a large number of workshops, seminars, and courses led by a varied group of knowledgeable users has permitted the study of how to make the approach flexible enough to accommodate differing temperaments and cultural conditions and the differing interests of teachers and now that a sufficient articulation of fundamental issues has been reached, it is possible to present in print a realistic discussion of the role of the teacher in the subordination of teaching to learning.

This we will do here. In the next chapter, we shall consider the question of how to increase the flow of teachers who know how to take advantage of what students bring to the classroom.

If a teacher is troubled by the apparent contradiction of ignorance in students, on the one hand, and, as I have maintained, the existence of enormous powers in their mind, on the other, he needs only to ask himself whether there is contradiction between the apparent staleness of matter and the amounts of energy that can be released from its transformation when we know how to perform this operation. He can also ask himself whether he ever uses any of the powers of the mind other than retention. If the answer is yes, then he may realize that by systematically emphasizing retention in the classroom, to the exclusion of the systematic use of any other power, he is the barrier that prevents the transformation from taking place.

There are four tasks facing a teacher who wants to subordinate teaching to learning. The first is *to become a person* who knows himself and others as persons. This is no mere sentimental homily, but means that a teacher must recognize that beyond any individual's behaviors is a *will* which changes behaviors and integrates them.

Though everyone knows the word will and even knows the "thing" it refers to, in our mechanistic approach to life we do not fully recognize its importance and significance.

Of all the powers of the mind, it is our will that permits us to become persons. On what basis can we make this statement? For one thing, the uniqueness of each of us, which is what makes us persons in contrast to specimens of a class of interchangeable beings—a worker, a soldier, a priest, etc.—is based on the fact that an individual can exert himself counter to any such classification. To be able to counter behaviors one has to reach that which generates behavior and maintains it. Our will is precisely that facet of our self that is present everywhere in our somatic-psychic system and can change us, stopping us from reaching out for a cigarette or from biting pencils or our nails, and generating the warnings that make a success of the stopping.

But our will is also present at moments when

there is no countering behaviors. The act of writing this page would clearly not take place in its detail if the hand was not directing at every instant the shaping of specific signs that correspond to words that correspond to thoughts that are brought forth and examined for their correspondence to the basic intention. Intention already contains a vector that foreshadows a will.

To utter any word we need to order vocal chords, lungs, vocal organs to form, according to the learned input, the right output.

The will is vigilant in its attention to our functionings, either correcting them or letting them pass by.

It is needed to do and *not* to do—to run away in a fire or to remain in a fire to save someone, to be silent or to talk, and so on.

Hence, if we want a notion that represents something that is as comprehensive as life, will is a happy choice. The will can serve to characterize the uniqueness of each of us: it constitutes the thing that can make the individual into a person.

Now, since in fact all our learning can be viewed as changed behaviors, when we use the will as a major notion, we have in this concept both the result and what causes it, the appearance and the reality—and the fundamental ally of teachers.

Seeing the students in our classrooms as persons, as endowed with a will that permits actions and generates by itself changes, we shall immediately be closer to them—closer to understanding each as a person and closer to helping each increase his experience and his understanding of it—for we shall have at our disposal what is indispensable for reaching any ends involving them. Attention is an outcome of the will. So is listening, and looking.

Without these signs of the working of the will, signs that the will is being mobilized for the tasks at hand, teachers are completely helpless.

In a perspective that views men as animals, the will is mobilized by threats of using against an individual greater force than he commanded. But there was no punishment that could completely blunt the will of some men, who as a result become saints, heroes, martyrs, symbols, and inspirations of people. So one can say at the very least that this view of man is incomplete.

In a perspective that views men as persons, results can be achieved by obtaining an individual's consent, cooperation, collaboration in working towards certain ends. Promises of spoils or rewards may suffice to obtain such an alliance. Contrary to the effect of punishment, rewards take us outside of ourselves, and move us into the fictitious or symbolic world of make-believe.

To speak of the agreement to mobilize oneself for some end brings us to a power of the mind discussed briefly in the last chapter, a power intimately linked to the will but distinguishable from it in its working: the power of producing images—which we will call *imaging* when we refer to the process of producing the actual images, and *imagination* when we stress content.

Imaging is a dynamic process of the mind in which mental energy is used *voluntarily* for some ends. For example, to be able to evoke a circle rather than something else when the word "circle" is uttered, is proof that this power of the mind exists. To evoke this image, however, means that not only the imaging power but the will must be employed. Thus, we can say that even voluntary imaging activities are deliberate, *willed* activities of the person, for each such activity could be countered. A distinction must be made here between men and animals. If a dog can evoke a bone as well as we do, it cannot evoke a new ballet for a particular company. Imaging and imagining nonetheless are powers that take one beyond the given, though the mental substance of which they are constituted may be of the same kind as that used by animals in their evokings. The difference lies in the working of man's will, which creates the not-given by its ability to counter it and is able to know that it did this.

So this is the first task of teachers, to know that they are persons with a will and that their students are persons with a will, and that in an individual, the will is the source of change.

The second task of the teacher is to acknowledge the existence of *a sense of truth* which guides us all and is the basis of all our knowing.

Since we all give proof of knowing so much before entering school, we also give proof of having mastered the criteria to take us through the by-us-unchartered world we are born into. It is in these criteria and through their elaboration in our own life that we can come to know our sense of truth and to use it consciously to conquer our cognitive universe.

For a tiger, a carrot has no nutritional value. Not so for a donkey. Our optical eye may produce an optical image on our retina or our brain, but its significance does not necessarily follow. Something else is required to give it significance; in animals, we call it instinct, in man sense. Until the image is accepted for its sense, it remains a suspended chunk of energy in the mind, to be dissolved if no sense is found in it, integrated if it is found meaningful. There is a higher instance in each of us that tells us that what we are perceiving is or is not real. This is our sense of truth, which functions well and independently at the beginning of life and less well in the instances when we have no immediate access to areas under investigation and we are made to lose our independence—the situation in the traditional classroom.

At school today teachers refer to the sense of truth either simplistically, as when they ask students to judge a situation by criteria they must accept as given, or deny its existence when they want students to make statements without ensuring that these statements are first meaningful to the students. An example of the first is the determination by a litmus test of whether or not a solution is acid; of the second, acceptance by the teacher's fiat of the rule that in French participles used with the verb "avoir" agree with the gender and number of objects when placed before it— particularly if the rule is put before students when they own little French.

Teachers can find that to be on the side of reality, they themselves have to use their own sense of truth. The more they are aware of it, the more they will find it in others and be able to make use of it to the advantage of all.

Here we shall list a number of situations that bring home how important it is to be aware of the sense of truth.

— Since each object can have as many names as there are languages, it is clear that nouns are conventions and in themselves are only a sound and cannot evoke images. Hence, we all learned to retain our native language when we noticed that our perceptions—which we cannot deny to ourselves—are labeled by our social environment in ways that are consistent even though arbitrary. Meaning carries the word; a word is retained because it evokes a meaning that one recognizes as true, and this alone—our own sense of truth—permits us to trust language and use it functionally.

— Our sense organs receive from the outer world impacts which are caused by energy reaching our system and affecting it somehow. Very early in our childhood, we recognize that affects on various organs can have sources that can be integrated, and we acknowledge, for example, that there is one person, whether we see her at a distance or very close in any of her garments, smell her when our eyes are shut, hear her respond to us from another room, feel her touch when she handles us, one person who is our mother. Inner criteria—an internal sense of truth—must exist to coordinate all this variety of impressions integrated into one overall objectivation, otherwise we would not be able to shift from one impression to another without losing contact with the truth that one person exists.

— Inner criteria is another way of knowing our sense of truth. A moment of reflection will make it clear to us that we have both direct and by-proxy experiences—that we hear words used by others to describe their experience (which comes to us by proxy) while we have words that emerge in our consciousness to describe some of our experiences (which we encountered directly). Direct experience not only gives the truth of our own living but provides us with the means to decide whether other people's experience is or is not true. If I said: "I went from New York City to San Francisco on my hands"—though the sentence is grammatically correct and evokes images that can be trusted, the content of the sentence is at once recognized as not true, on the basis of personal experience, by all those who can make sense of the words.

Our sense of truth is called upon constantly whether we live directly or by-proxy, at school no less than at home or in the street. It accompanies us as the flashlight in the dark that knits perceptions into knowledge of where to go and what to avoid.

Clearly, if we know how to remain in contact with our own sense of truth during our meetings with students, they will understand what we are offering them and take responsibility for the integration of this knowledge in their self, which is how they proceeded in their spontaneous life until then. But if we do not suspect that the absence of inner criteria hinders retention and if we offer statements to be remembered per se, we end up with students who answer questions like "2 plus 3?" by another question—"Five?"—and wait for confirmation by the teacher.

When we consider all knowing and all knowledge, we find another aspect of the sense of truth.

We see that there are questions that can be answered with certainty (assuming that the words of the questions are known and understood) by all. Questions such as: "Is it raining?" "Is the sun out?" "Is Peter here?"

There are also questions reducible to the immediate situation for an answer: "Are there forty people here?"—a count, if carefully carried out, will provide the answer; "Is this lady that boy's mother?"—and investigation would provide an answer: "Is this green stuff on that slice of bread dew or mold?"—a microscopic examination and a comparative photograph would settle the matter, or create a new research problem.

But there are some questions that cannot be answered by recourse to the immediate. Some of them are without much significance: "Was there a woman on the right of Nero when Rome burnt?" "Did Napoleon start walking with his left foot on June 16, 1815?" Some are significant: "How could so many men believe for so long that the earth was flat?" "What is the real shape of the earth?" For the significant questions to be investigated may require new awarenesses no one can foresee. Some questions become significant as man allows them to teach him their meanings: "Is poverty inevitable?" "What is the role of the brain in intellectual activity?"

Thus, we can see that different kinds of questions demand different activities from us and in some instances necessitate that we expand our awareness. So it is with our students. Just as for us to understand means to let the phenomenon in question force our mind to take it into account, so for the students in our schools understanding is the enlargement of the awareness so as to make sense of what is contemplated.

Without the existence of a sense of truth, we cannot comprehend why men would want to understand anything and in some cases pay a high price in terms of energy consumption and time for understanding it.

What is superficially termed curiosity is the meeting between the reality around us with the sense of truth within us.

The third task of the teacher is to find out *how knowing becomes knowledge.*

Since this problem applies to himself as well as to all others, what he needs to do is watch himself making this transformation. A key moment, a key notion. At once he will find that there are a number of ways of knowing and that knowledge covers a spectrum of meanings. First there is the knowing that happens by merely letting a sensibility be connected with reality. For example: light and sound reach us and affect us. Thus to know if "it" is blue or yellow, one only needs to open one's eyes and the energy of the photons will do the rest. The knowledge comes from a recognized property of the impact. Knowing here is yielding our senses to reality, and knowledge is the result of a specific adaptation of the receiving system to the incident rays.*

But we are knowers not simply because our somatic substance can be affected by energy but also because once energy is absorbed, we can keep some of its structural attributes as they come to us. How do we know this? Because we manage to perceive that there is a characteristic quanta of energy to photons. We manage to perceive whether a given photon (or a bunch of them) has once before reached us or not. This is another way of knowing, in which an evocation of prior impacts leads to another awareness: whether the present impact is new. Our mind knows this is the case or not, and in knowing this, our sense of truth is functioning. Because there is an evocation simultaneously with the holding of the impact (after it has been received), the comparison of what is with what was becomes a way of knowing— one aspect of what can properly be called the functionings of memory when this way of knowing

---

*This cursory study cannot exhaust the subject in question, particularly because the presentation, to be brief, uses words that are ambiguous and raise questions by themselves. Readers who continue reading will find many observations that will act as correctives to the first picture offered at this stage.

becomes sufficiently extended to hold a large
number of impacts and inner adaptations.

From the start of any of our functionings, there
was a need and the possibility of distinguishing
every present moment from all others. Such
comparisons led to the ways of knowing that we
earlier called "stressing and ignoring" because they
involved a polarization of the mind in which there
was awareness of some things that made for
similarities or differences but not of other things.
This particular awareness led to another, which was
that our mind can indeed stress and ignore at will
and systematically, that this operation was a way
of knowing.

The fact that these ways of knowing are known
by the mind as its own powers is grasped after
they are used spontaneously and have become part
of the fabric of living. To reach them requires that
we become aware of our own awareness at work.

All our students have developed these ways of
knowing, which have served them well as the basis
for the learning they accomplished alone—through
their own contact with their soma learning to turn,
to sit, to stand, to make and recognize sounds, to
grasp, to walk, to speak their environmental
language, to climb, to jump, to run, to open their
hands, to close them, to brush, to dress, to wash,
etc.

All small children know that to achieve mastery
in any skill they must concentrate, avoid
distractions, and practice until they have all the
required functionings so smoothly integrated that
they work as if by themselves, as if the activity was
second nature.

Each skill may require a different way of
knowing. And each skill ends up by being a

know-how, which is a kind of knowledge that does not seem related to the outside world.

Now, school people have put the stress on the kind of knowledge that is not a know-how. They insist rather on seeking to impart knowledge that can be verbalized and transmitted verbally, and everything they attempt to import is treated as if it were knowledge of this sort. To traditional teachers, the Pythagorean theorem seems very little like a know-how; rather it seems to them an example of pure knowledge that one can own only if traditional transmission has taken place. Between the Pythagorean theorem and the date of the Battle of Gettysburg, they see only shades of knowledge, no differences of kind—all this knowledge to be retained, of course, by repetition and other forms of memorization. To such teachers, lack of knowledge is a sign of a weak memory or the lack of application in the effort to remember.

Similarly, there are psychopedagogical theories that ignore all ways of knowing except the one that rests on drill and repetition.

Obviously, if we remain in contact with reality, with the various ways we ourselves have developed our sense of truth, we are not persuaded that traditional understanding is an adequate picture of how learning takes place. This is why we must study how knowing becomes in ourselves (and in others we are teaching) investigating how we learned to speak our native language or how many exercises we needed to do to know how to climb steps or a chair or a tree.

Teachers have a fourth task, the duty to consider the *economy of learning.*

No reasonable person will agree to pay thirty thousand dollars for an ordinary 1955 Chevrolet, but in schools it often seems that teachers and curriculum specialists are prepared to let students pay amounts of time equivalent to thirty thousand dollars for merchandise equivalent to such a car.

Indeed time, which for every individual is the stuff of his life, is not considered by teachers as having any value. Teachers are prepared to repeat and repeat, review and review, correct and correct, as many times as they face a given group of students. Since they are being paid for their time, one can say that they are receiving a return for it (though the return they are getting may not be the full return they could get), but it does not seem that their students get any return at all, for the knowledge that is to be gotten in exchange for the time spent by the students eludes most of them.

A reflection on the acts of living will show us that to live is to change time into experience. So time must be considered as what we are endowed with by the act of coming into the world and that the consumption of time, if it is not to be destructive for the individual, should lead to some equivalent worth in terms of experience, which when accumulated, becomes growth.

All of us, at least as children, have always known how to change time into experience, and some of us have found how to transform it into special experiences with different kinds of specific attributes (such as lasting, ephemeral, social, religious, mystic, etc.).

The way of knowing that permits us to compare our transformations of time into experiences—and, say, rank one as better than another—includes aspiring and inspiration. Through utilization of these powers, mankind has produced groups of people who transform time in similar ways, ways which then became values for these people and molded the education provided in these groups. But it has not been recognized that education cannot take place until an awareness exists of the particular awareness that a group values, and students have been asked to pay any price in time to obtain the valued knowledge, even if the process made them unable to use time properly and crippled them in a number of areas.

For the spontaneous transformation of time into experience is not necessarily social. In their first few days in the world, extra-utero babies are not even concerned with the physical environment. Similarly, in the first years of our life, none of us seeks employment and independent economic support. Rather, then as it should be always, the individual knows what he is equipped to work on and applies himself to master what can be reached, thereby making himself competent to attack related fields.

Teachers can learn by watching these spontaneous transformations, which are the laws of the economy of life, and should make them their allies rather than work counter to them and help change students into rebels and dropouts.

The economics of education as such is quite simple. It resembles the economics of everyday spontaneous life: students' time must buy equivalent experience. Good teaching can act on time as well as experience, for psychological time has a component of *intensity* that clock time lacks, and this intensity may distinguish by its presence two lived seconds, minutes, hours, or days, in which what the time can buy as its equivalent may be enhanced, widened, deepened, and made to reach further.

What is new in all this discussion of the tasks for the teacher who wants to subordinate teaching to learning, is the inclusion of the student as a person, endowed with a working sense of truth which keeps him in contact with reality, which he knows as it demands to be known and the knowledge of which he owns because he has paid the correct price to acquire it. In this context, teaching becomes a new activity originating within the complex of "knowing-people" who meet deliberately for the explicit purpose of changing time into experience with the greatest efficiency possible.

The inclusion of the student as a person is indeed a new concept which cannot be reduced to inspired teaching anymore than to traditional teaching. It amounts to nothing less than the science of education in operation, guaranteed to work because it takes into account the true components of the situation and neglects none of them through bias or preconceptions. It is the one way of seeing what is and of working with what is.

In this approach, the teacher in a classroom is there only because he qualifies for the unique job he has to do. Since he has lived and knows firsthand how to change time into experience, he will be able to concentrate on the specific, particular duties imposed on him by the unique composition of his class of students in the concrete, which he sees not solely in terms of their age or the grade curriculum, the ambitions of their parents, or the values of the environment. All these have their place in the reality of the situation, but they do not determine the fundamental task: effective change of the students' time into experiences that are true and meaningful to them *now*.

For teachers to work this way alters their role as much as it alters their preparation.

Without introducing the substantive question of what education should consist of (the subject of all the proposals that seek to make education resemble the ideal of their authors), it is possible to consider the impact upon traditional classroom work of an approach in which teaching is subordinated to learning.

A teacher who acts as a person among other persons cannot forget his students and only stress covering the material of the official syllabus or curriculum, or only stress the length of the period, or only think of testing and grades, or only spend his time doing to others what was done to him. On the contrary, he will marvel at the masteries shown by his students in so many fields and ask himself how any one of the tasks officially handed to him as his school duty compares in difficulty with what his students have already proved capable of doing. He will ask himself how he can use the powers of the children so as to enable these students to master the prescribed tasks and will go on to question how he can use the time available to him to expand the range of tasks before the students and, in so far as the school's fields of study are specific skills (reading, mathematics, etc. but not, for example, social sciences), help the students master them.

Every one of us enters school knowing how to be a responsible learner, an independent investigator, an autonomous judge of what is his

The Subordination of Teaching to Learning

immediate interest and how to go about one's
own duties to oneself as one's self-conception
dictates.

But every one of us has only investigated what
the environment and family circumstances permit.
A school is a contrived milieu created by adults so
that what is not offered spontaneously by life can
be offered as fields of study that can extend the
reaches of everyone.

If children came to school reading, reading
would not be taught, anymore than in normal
schools walking is taught.

If children came to school capable of operating
on whole numbers and fractions, elementary
arithmetic would not be offered.

Schools are but one of the instruments devised
by men to prepare their children for their future
tasks and challenges. They are not supposed to
repeat the functions of homes and streets, and for
those students who have homes and streets the
function of schools should be special, unique. (For
the students who do not have home or street,
schools can add to themselves some functions that
will serve as substitutes for the missing sources of
experience.)

Hence we may postulate that the contrived
curriculum of schools in which teaching is
subordinated to learning would take into clear
account all of what children know and not bother
to repeat it but on the contrary would deliberately
offer extensions of one's awareness of the three
universes of experience—the inner, the natural, and
the human—so as to help the student continue his
mastery of himself, his domination of nature
through increased knowledge of its workings and
his understanding of the variety of human

68

experience, all of which everyone takes to school when he joins it.

Because we do not have to teach either responsibility or autonomy, if we continue to play in our work the same games that children played spontaneously before attending school, nor have to take the time to show how to make sense of the various worlds we live in (which the children already know), as teachers in such a situation we start much better off than those who give to schools all sorts of jobs, including ones already catered for.

There are schools today where the dominating concern is the inculcation and development of responsibility. Their focus is on social actions and a socially pervaded reality. There are schools where the dominating note is the development of autonomy. Their focus is on the area of human relationships that have been made confused for their students by individuals who did not recognize that people at different moments of their life ignore different aspects of it and stress others and who forced children unprepared into a layer of life still to come.

But the role of teachers becomes clearer and more true to a teacher's fundamental tasks if as adults they acknowledge that *relativity* is demanded by their function and that they must transcend the dominance o{ any particular viewpoint represented in society by groups living out further some special human possibility. Naturally, young teachers are still totally engaged in exploring the world, and some older ones choose not to transcend theirs. Neither of these types of people can truly subordinate teaching to learning, which demands relativity or absolute acceptance

that we are different, are called by our present
condition to explore particular universes, and are
at every point of our life truly taken by our
explorations, which tint all we do or think.

As we saw earlier, relativity is the name for the
awareness that all moments in one's life are
equivalent (of equal value), that all lives are
meaningful, that to understand another person is
to examine universes from different systems of
reference and to uncover the transformations that
make them look as they do.

Still, to understand others as they are is not
sufficient to become a true teacher for them. One
also has to know how to look on their present
activities so as to expand their consciousness of the
world and of themselves.

For instance, to restate in this context some of
our previous discussion, the role of the teacher of
reading of the native language is to provide his
students with what is needed to transform a
functioning spoken speech into a functioning
written speech. This may be done, as I have
indicated, easily and quickly.

The role of the teacher of mathematics is to
recognize that a student who can speak has a
large number of mental structures which can serve
as the basis for awarenesses that will enable him to
transform these structures into mathematical ones.
In particular, algebra, defined as operations upon
operations, is already the endowment of all
students of all ages and to work from it will make
every child into a budding mathematician. In such
an approach, mathematics teaching becomes the
task of making students aware of themselves as the
basis of reaching the dynamics of mathematical
relationships and of offering them the situations

that involve all sorts of these relationships. (The difference in the levels of the students will be acknowledged not in the type of problem posed for them but only through the components of the situations offered them, for example, geoboards with nails and rubberbands for the beginners, and the group of the seventeen plane symmetries for the more advanced ones.*)

The role of the teacher of social studies is first to recognize the level of a student's social awareness and then to provide him with the means of entering into ways of living followed by other people (who may be from his own environment or from another) so that words about these people evoke correct imagery which would be functional for the student if he were to visit the people. Young students can enter lives of other people through their appearance and some of their folklore, older students through their actions and their institutions, still older ones through a study of what may follow social actions of certain kinds and of how to acquire social maturity. Social studies in schools differ from social living at home and in the streets by the inclusion of relativity, systematic questioning, serious collection of data, and examination of issues of all sorts whether they concern one's case or not. A teacher of social studies who is involved in relativity as other citizens are involved in present-day issues will generate in his students: respect for truth in a field not always open to the sense of truth; the sensitivity of students; an understanding that place and

---

*I have laid out a course of mathematics covering many years in *Mathematics with Numbers in Colour* Vol. I to Vol. VII. Available from: Educational Solutions Inc., 821 Broadway, New York, N.Y. 10003.

time have a role to play in people's living; humility, as one encounters foolishness and greatness side by side in so many places and times; sympathy for he who tries and does not succeed and for those who chose worthy attitudes that lead to disaster; and so on.

The teacher of physical education, because he comes into contact with somas already highly dominated by the will, is fulfilling his true function when he takes his charges towards deeper awareness of their embodiment in their physical activities of energy and will acting upon energy systems, through such study helping them do what lies within their capabilities to do, which may well be beyond present thresholds of achievement.

The teacher of music is one who knows that the first instrument is in our throat and is directly accessible to the self. On this basis, he can give his students access to the music each carries and from there lead them to the awareness of the world of sound both as it can be studied in acoustics and as musicians have made it look. To own music is something else than to know pieces or even how to play an instrument. It is rather, as an example, the awareness that one is a vibrating system capable of resonance, of organizing in different time sequences sounds that one can produce through one's pneumatic or muscular actions upon other vibrating systems.

All these roles can be carried out in any classroom in the world if the relationship of teacher and student is one of a gift of each to the other. The immense universe of man's experience, which by its sheer vastness inspires us, will inspire student and teacher alike. If teachers technically know how to take advantage of all the ways of

72

knowing present in their students, the outcome *is* subordination of teaching to learning, a know-how for teachers that they will come to own as all other know-hows are learned, through trial and error, practice and mastery.

Our contact with ourselves being continuous, we have developed a way of keeping record of all we do in our soma and with our soma, psyche, and will. This type of relating is made of a grid of feedback mechanisms.

Our contact with our work in schools can be developed on a similar pattern which replaces the "at-the-end" test by instruments that continuously inform teachers of what continuously is occurring in everyone in their classrooms. To achieve this, the instruments must be integrated in the teaching itself and in the materials used for such teaching. What are such instruments? They include:

— silence on the part of the teacher, so that he can clearly hear the verbal messages of the students,

— worksheets that can be returned to the student and kept rather than thrown away; which can provide the student with a picture of the progress he has made since he completed a particular class,

— individual and group work, where one compares one's attempts at mastery, invention, etc., with what others have done during the same period.

To sum up: the role of a teacher in a school that subordinates teaching to learning will always be one of a knower, of an active person meeting other persons on fields of study which challenge him as well as them, his students.

Such a teacher will invent new techniques every

time he becomes aware that another way to enter a particular field exists for himself or for some of his students. He will never consider that a predetermined program can do this unique job of the encounter of person and person.

He will not believe that any knowledge can be beyond revision or is independent of all knowers; hence he will receive all knowledge as the outcome of some way of knowing which involves more than the knowledge.

In the next chapter, a study of the education of teachers for the subordination of teaching to learning will add much to what we have put into circulation on the role of the teacher so far.

5.

Preliminaries to the Science of Education*

Since teachers are prepared for their jobs at colleges and at university departments of education, an important potential source of change in schools are the teachers of teachers. They will become agents for change when they:

    — recognize that a new approach to classroom work is more effective on the whole than the approach they are presenting, but still produces what they believe should be accomplished by their professional activities, and

    — find that the new approach is not too costly in their own personal terms.

In this chapter we shall demonstrate that it is reasonable to expect teachers of teachers to join the ranks of those who are succeeding in giving education new means to perform its tasks.

We shall also examine seriously a number of issues important not only for teachers of teachers

---

*A more extended publication devoted to this subject will be published in the near future.

but also for ordinary citizens baffled by what goes on in our societies all over the world.

While everybody in a college of education knows what goes wrong in such and such a course, very few participants can do anything about the problems they are aware of because the main trouble comes from the very fragmentation of interwoven material into separate courses and the failure to see that education is concerned with persons and not with atoms of knowledge.

It is conceivable that if the faculty of a college were motivated to look at the whole of what goes on in their institution, they would not hesitate to make all the efforts that would be necessary to implement one or more changes from which all might benefit.

Were this to happen, it would be a good example of an identity between self-interest and the common good. If we can agree that most people are moved by the first and that the second is generally regarded as desirable, then we can be guided by the notion that while we cannot ask for a sacrifice in the name of an ideal, we perhaps can obtain it in the name of the first, the true mover of man. Here the sacrifice that is required is a gift of one's time to seriously consider whether what is suggested in this text can reconcile effectively self-interest and the needs of the common good.

Every reader will therefore decide for himself whether the proposals made here meet with his idea of himself, of his personal success, of his role in the world.

As a test of coherence, the writer, who is a teacher and a teacher of teachers, will strive to be precise in detail and comprehensive enough in presentation so as to include all those who, while they may differ from him, can still come to see their interest respected in almost every one of the statements made in this book.

Teachers of teachers not only have to reach their own students, but beyond them, those whom these students will meet in their future classrooms. While it may seem unreasonable to talk about the second (absent) group of students in considering the role of the teachers of teachers, it would be an error to ignore the first who are present.

The idea of teaching teachers as one would wish them to teach students is attractive and has been diversely developed over the centuries. But because so many of the student teachers are expected to teach a body of material they presumably have come to know, the preparation of teachers can break down as soon as the student teacher recognizes that his case is not being taken into account, that while he is being asked to find out what he knows, *his* students will have to meet what they do not know.

Hence so long as we are being prepared to teach by trying to discover what we already know (however scantly), we cannot be helped to find out how to teach it to one who does not yet have access to it. And in those instances in which we are meeting what we do not know, we are engaged in the act of knowing and can rarely notice the procedure that leads to knowledge and then benefit by this awareness for the future.

Perhaps so far in education, by concentrating on knowledge, we have been stressing not very useful aspects of the fabric of teaching. The inconclusive controversy between content and procedure may teach us that we have to raise ourselves one or two rungs higher so as to embrace at the same time these presumably distinct elements and integrate them into a wider whole.

For instance, if we knew what is educable in us, we might have access to a notion that is valid for all of us at all ages, to be met in one context when we consider children at various moments of their life at school, and in another when we specialize in the education of teachers who have to know how children can be educated.

Let us assume that the writer is asked to work with a number of teachers of teachers to demonstrate what he means when he looks for this flexible and comprehensive notion that nonetheless is sufficiently precise to become a tool for all educators. What can he communicate in writing about such a demonstration workshop?

The unstructured features of the situation described here—which draws on the actual seminar technique used by the writer when working with educators—will serve as a guarantee that this approach is transferable to other groups.

The relationship of the leader of the seminar and the participants is one of *equality in ignorance.* But respect of every person does not reduce itself to the acceptance of any statement made by any individual. One may find that an individual is emotionally attached to a statement. On the contrary, very soon the difference between fact and opinion becomes clear: everything stated stands or falls on its own because of the truth it contains or lacks.

For instance, no one is allowed to speak on behalf of all, or in fact for anyone other than himself, before finding whether his statement does indeed apply to anyone other than himself. "We" is replaced by "I."

Another way to alert participants to the difference between fact and opinion is to have them use the plural instead of the universal: "children" instead of "the child," "teachers" instead of "the teacher."

A question used freely from the start is: "How do you know?" or "How would one know this?" This question has the power of throwing people back to their evidence to find if it is sufficient or wanting.

In fact, what is done by the opening technique of the seminar is more than alert people and, in effect, make them doubt all they believe until it is satisfactorily proved to them that criteria exist to judge whether one is holding opinion or speaking the "truth." For when this point is reached, participants have no fear anymore of being brought to the realization that some or much of all they believe needs revision and strengthening. They are even grateful for being opened to this awareness and are ready to contribute creatively to a study placed in front of them.

The theme of any study is at first far less important than the approach to the theme. Therefore any theme is useful so long as it is capable of arousing the participants to questioning their own habits of thought and ways of knowing.

Among questions that have such a quality, we can include the following:

— Is the earth really round? What does this mean?

— Does anyone here really know what one

79

does in order to stand up from a sitting position? ("Really" is the key word of the question.)

    — Do words have meaning of their own?

    — Does anyone know whether we can learn by imitation? What does this mean?

    — Is this body of mine my body? In what sense?

    — What do babies do soon after birth? How could we know?

    — Who is to tell educators what they should do? Where does the authority of "authorities" come from?

Because these questions have roots in everyone's experience, it is possible to engage all participants in the examination of the challenge they pose. The leader of the seminar does not have to be able to give set answers to these or the many other questions that come to mind. All he has to do is keep the participants at work on the question until either a solution is proposed that appears to satisfy the critical powers of the group or until new problems emerge which require attention and then to shift the group's attention to one of them. What there is to learn through the exchange is how to handle problems as they emerge, not how to find answers that enable one to run away from them.

At first every participant will find that a particular question is or is not challenging. Those who find it challenging will be mobilized to reflect, to look around in their own mind whether the words evoke any meaning. Those who are accustomed to answering quickly may say something to the point, either meaningful or trivial. Both sorts of participants can be given the leader's attention who through a counter-example can perhaps force the second to examine again what he said, and by asking "How does one know this?" may elicit from the first an elaboration of the contribution he has made.

When such techniques are used:

— a serious investigative spirit can be fostered;

— all participants contribute to the study (even if they say nothing) by watching the progress that is made in handling the questions under investigation and by seeing how more light is shed on the topics considered;

— no participant wishes anymore to score a point but wants rather to clarify issues, becoming demanding of oneself and others, with the result that the discussion moves ahead rather than serves a personal purpose;

— the fragmentation that results from analyses is replaced by integration of facets, since the relevance of serious viewpoints is accepted implicitly (because of the respect accorded to everyone's experience) and since everyone attempts to avoid irrelevancies and waste of time;

— the end not being a final authoritative statement but a pregnant formulation of what every reality may be formed of, participants leave discussions with a multitude of stimulating challenges which require further examination and the test of reality.

In this way people become activated and see that the future is promising rather than sterile, that one will find no end to one's findings. Such seminars have been acknowledged as a life-giving experience. One feels the need for many co-workers to really tackle large issues and, at the same time, the confidence that inner criteria exist which make one an independent authority in knowing what is valuable and what needs to be pursued first.

81

In the context of a seminar with educators, let
us consider how we would deal with the question:
what is educable in us?

Putting this question will at first have the effect
of generating a blank in the group discussing it,
since as educators we all take for granted that we
always knew the answer, even though we never
thought of it, just by virtue of the fact that we are
in education.

To help the group in the examination of the
matter, we can place it in front of very difficult
questions, such as: is our brain educable? Or: is
memory educable?

The pursuit of these two questions will depend
on who forms the group, but soon we shall need to
be clearer on the matter of what we mean by
educable. Does it mean "improved," and does this
apply to memory even if it does not apply to the
brain? Or does it mean "functioning better" for
some specific purposes? And what would this
specifically mean in the case of the brain or of
memory?

Our brain is one of the most difficult areas of
study for scientists at the present time and even if
we can be acquainted with much of the brain's
anatomy and histology, there is little to guide lay
people in the field of physiology, since neurologists
are still trying to agree with each other on which
are the basic problems to work on first in the study
of the brain, and which are the reliable methods.

(Even if we were better informed about the
functionings of the brain, we would not find
neurologists who accept the proposition, which I
can do no more than state here, that our brain is
subordinated to a higher biological entity that
could change the functionings. To neurologists, our

brain is the highest entity and commands the rest of life in each of us. What brain specialists study is the brain's functionings, and these only "improve" because of "evolution," which is the general biological process of change.)

Memory is not easier to handle though it can more easily become the object of anecdotes and more easily escapes the rigor of scientific research.

Is an improved memory one which retains more? more easily? at a rate defined as the amount retained per unit of time? Or is memory improved when it retains selectively? in other words, allows us to pass through irrelevant material thrown at us at random by the world around us?

Discussion along such lines could help us in knowing what we individually mean by educable, since it would give us notions that pull our mind in different directions. Relevancy (in the case of brain and the question of how to study it) and retention (in the case of memory) would be seen as variables and not as pure notions. As a result, values are felt to underlie the evocation of these terms and so at once the complexity of the matter is experienced. Such realization is a welcome feature of these seminars, one that opens the future to questions rather than to the attempt to find answers that close discussions.

For anyone in these discussions who discovers that he has accepted many opinions without serious examination, the critical sense seems to be one of the first educable traits that one can reach. Indeed, if one was generally not critical of anything one heard proposed authoritatively, and then becomes capable of questioning such assertions, one in fact has changed. This inner transformation is experienced (properly) as an education simply because one is aware both of oneself and of how one relates to statements that are presented as true but may only be opinion.

It is easy to draw parallels from this awareness to any number of fields. For example, if on some day one found that from not being able to drive a car, one could now take it onto the highways, something must have happened to oneself.

Such examples are legion. One passes from not being able to read, or write, or do arithmetical operations to the state when each is second nature.

We can now ask: do these changes involve separate educable traits or is there in all of the changes that which indeed is educable in us?

Looking at ourselves involved in various acts of learning makes us sensitive to the self that is educable and that holds the outcome of education. Rather than something that has been added to oneself as a quantity, education is a quality, a state of being that is found to consist of knowing rather than knowledge. Once this is recognized, one sees clearly that knowledge exists per se outside of us while knowing occurs within us and is identified with us.

The question, what is educable in us? takes us back to ourselves and puts to everyone a question answerable only by each person. It is then possible to see that each of us has always known that what is educable in us required our personal attention. We had in us the best teacher, the one who, though only a second ahead of his pupil, knew exactly what to do to take the pupil from not knowing to knowing and then through a special awareness to knowledge.

But awareness is a universe, not one thing reached all at once and forever. Because of this, education is a never-ending task, an ever-renewed challenge taking us from one peak to a new departure to climb again to a new peak and so on.

In spite of the fact that we can see knowledge accumulating, we all have to build the whole of our own education from scratch. No one can experience for us. We need to undertake on our own every one of the steps that lead to mastery. This is both a curse and a blessing: a curse because it prevents us from saving time where others have spent it, a blessing because it permits us to continuously remold the world and make it more adequate to what we find in it—for example, make the schools more adequate to the existing powers of children.

If we want to describe the process of education in terms of knowledge and its display in books and other documents, then to educate is to make one benefit from what others have met and ascertained. But even this can only happen when we change our time (to scan pages in books or perform any other activity required by the field of study) into the acts of learning and making sense—that is, into becoming aware of some reality.

Thus, whether we start from knowledge or knowing, we reach awareness as the necessary notion in the answer to "what is educable in us?".

Having found this, we now have a multitude of new jobs which may need generations of workers to make them explicit and to use them with certainty in the institutions now called schools.

So at the end of such a seminar—which we offer here as a model of the themes and approaches by which teachers can be prepared to enter their profession equipped to subordinate teaching to learning—a new life begins for the participants who have been stirred, who see that a number of tasks and problems are waiting for them:

— How does awareness create its own mental tools to apprehend reality as revealed by this awareness?

— Can one be so totally absorbed in an activity—that is to say, in one's activity—that one misses becoming aware that one is aware?

— Is it necessary to reach awareness of one's awareness before one can affect the various awarenesses of the multiple aspects of the world?— in particular, for becoming an agent of change in the world?

— If this is found to be the case, can one educate one's capacity to be aware of awareness in such a way that one never leaves what is educable in us and still remains in contact with the various facets of awareness of the actual world?

With these questions, we come to a second aspect of the teaching of teachers, for each and all of these questions go to form the fabric of *the science of education.*

Science is a study of some awarenesses that propose challenges to which men find answers when they create the appropriate tools for solution. These tools reflect the level of awareness of the challenge. Like the challenges, the instruments of science are expressible in terms of awareness.

In case of education, the awarenesses to be studied are the phenomena of awareness itself. Hence, the educators working on this will find themselves the scientists of the day. What do their tools consist of? All the necessary studies can be carried out either by working on oneself through seminars like those mentioned above, or in special experiments specifically conceived to clarify a matter encountered in one's awareness. There will, in any case, no longer be a need for the so-called "control-group experiments," which have taught us nothing, because a challenge in education always consists of discovering how uniquely people handle themselves in certain circumstances.

When it became known in nuclear physics that the instruments affect the observations they record, it became necessary, so as to gain the most precise information, to choose which of a number of components of a situation one studied. In psychology we have been faced with a similar challenge: observers affect observations. However complicating this may be, in order to reach subatomic or psychological reality, we have to be reconciled to these facts.

In education, since we are working on awarenesses, we must leave to each self the job of asserting, in one of a number of ways, what is happening—that is, leave to each his own awarenesses.

Thus, statements in the science of education will be true only if made in the plural and when using cautionary words such as "some," "sometimes," "possibly," etc. The statements will then strike everyone as possibly true. They could also be formulated in terms of the set of the people satisfying them. For example: "Those who are not blind or unable to see and have managed to learn to speak to the satisfaction of their environment, can learn to read at the age of four or later, in a matter of weeks."

Such a statement is conditional, but within these conditions it specifies that the only readiness required for success in mastering written speech is to be able to perceive it and to own enough of the spoken language to make sense of words. No other condition is included in the stated fact, though obviously the word *can* is there to balance the motivation factor. Since awareness is required to read (as it is in order to learn any other activity), distractions work counter to it. Eliminating distractions so that awareness is made possible will yield effectively the power to read.

"Reading is no longer a problem," a statement made in this book, is one of the statements the science of education has made possible. Today we know all we need to know to make with certainty such statements. But we must recognize that for anyone who does not conceive of the task of reading in terms of awareness, it may still be a problem—an insoluble one at that, because if we are not concerned with awareness, we do not work on what is educable in us so as to come to own reading after a time of not owning it.

What this example stresses is the possibility today of embarking upon some important studies in education and of coming up with valid answers just as we did and do in physics, chemistry, or mathematics.

Research plays a part in the preparation of teachers, so here we provide a list of possible educational topics that can be investigated in schools or colleges as is done in the schools that teach the exact sciences. To provide a useful list we shall sacrifice extension to detail and choose areas that allow us to say enough to be of help at once.

General readers may wish to skip the next few pages, which necessarily must deal with a number of special matters, and rejoin the discussion for the concluding section. Yet the list, in a skeletal fashion, does elaborate on the central challenge of learning, and so may contain something of general interest.

I.   In the area of reading, the following are among the most promising themes for an extensive and potentially profound research to be carried out by teams of investigators on college faculties:

1.   How do very young children manage to abstract words when they only hear voices?

2.   What is the control system used by very young children to be sure of producing the sounds they hear?

3.   What are the particular demands made on the minds of children by the various grammatical categories they master in order to use their native language as adults in their environment do? Here a gross classification—nouns, pronouns, adjectives, etc.—will lead to a number of more shaded distinctions, leading to more and more detailed study of the demands thereby ultimately enabling adults to find out how children do learn to speak.

4.   How do children retain words which are arbitrary signs generally accepted without examination by most adults?

5.   When do babies solve the problem of the sound sequences that go to form words? And why don't they mix inverse or very close sequences?

6.   What is the role of melody in a language in conveying its meanings, helping one's retention of it, and proposing mental habits that go to form one's mode of thought?

7.   What is the relative importance of the awareness of time to that of space in learning to read?

8. What is the role of the selection of the "restricted languages" in developing a progressive approach to the exhaustive study of reading by various natives?

9. What is the hierarchy of demands made on the mind by the various aspects of reading (conventions, decoding, fluent reading, and comprehension; reading for information, reading for acquiring knowledge, reading for edification, reading for acquiring experience by proxy, reading for inspiration, reading for the study of the language, reading for entertainment, and so on), and which parts of the self are being mobilized in each?

10. What are the means to accelerate the various phases of the learning sequences? What is the role of television in such acceleration?*

11. What is the optimal reading speed in relation to the differing levels of difficulty in the texts read.

12. What is necessary for a realistic attack on illiteracy so that: reading is assured to first graders; total remediation is provided in elementary schools; mastery of the various forms of speech (including spelling and grammatical correctness) is achieved at secondary school levels; and accelerated remediation is provided for dropouts and adults?

13. How can comparative phonetics be made available for all, along with reading in a second or further language? (For this, a vast study using computers may provide a breakthrough in the field of language study and teaching.)

14. What is added and what is lost when separating auditory from visual components in communicating through speech? (Teaching reading

*The author has dealt with the second question in his previous study, *Towards a Visual Culture: Educating Through Television* (New York: Outerbridge and Dienstfrey, 1969).

to the blind and to the deaf may benefit from such studies.)

II. In the area of mathematics, the following themes will contribute a great deal in clarifying issues on which there now exists only confused opinions:

1. Precisely what preparation for the study of mathematics do we find in our having learned to speak? How early are speakers equipped to enter into a dialogue with mathematics? How can we take advantage at various levels of the "mathematical readiness" given to children in their mastery of speech? For example, is it possible to provide as exercises for small children the structuration of situations in place of the usual exercises of so-called elementary notions?

2. Awareness of relationships per se is what distinguishes mathematical from all other thinking. Is it possible to offer a complete mathematics curriculum in terms of awareness? Is it possible to replace the linear presentation of mathematical ideas by a variety of entries into the field, all starting from scratch and each calling for special awarenesses, and have our students reach at least as good a grasp of mathematics as is currently attained by the best learners?

3. Starting with learners being deliberately engaged in entertaining some kinds of dialogues with contrived situations, which are the awarenesses that lead to mathematical statements and to the certainty of their truth.

4. If mathematics is taught through awareness, can one transfer findings made in the area of mathematics to other fields?

5. Mathematical logics are sets of specialized awarenesses of the dynamics of reducing ideas or of constructing them from simpler ones. Can we account for various schools of logic in terms of

varying awareness? What are the essential differences in awareness that characterize the various large mathematical structures that go to form the chapters of modern mathematics? Can we see a person's varying logical needs in terms of the way he organizes mental experience? Does one become more demanding when one thinks of counter-examples more easily (i.e., has more experience of a fluctuating universe)?

6. Visual perception being linked with our sense of truth, to what extent do we gain conviction about mathematical truths from our perceptions?

7. Imagery is part of geometrical thinking. How can we master the dynamics of imagery? Is it possible to give everyone the adequate basis for excelling in geometry through a study of what images can do for us?

8. Does algebraic thinking do away with images? Is algebraic mental behavior a sui generis use of one's mind needed for all transformational thinking, including that which uses imagery? What is the place of algebra in learning to speak or read? In other learnings?

9. Is there need for a new epistemology to account for the style of learning displayed by those who become mathematicians?

10. If a new epistemology is required to describe the actual ways of knowing used by young children to acquire, say, their mastery of numbers, can we accelerate learning of all by using this epistemology as a basis for teaching?*

11. What can we learn in looking at the unfolding of mathematics in time from the viewpoint of awareness? Does it reveal itself as a process in which naive positions are replaced by

---

*See the Appendix, "Notes on a New Epistemology."

more sophisticated ones? If so, what does this mean?

12. Since mathematics has a future, one that must be presumed unknown, to respect the future here means to ask questions of this kind: what have been the sources of mathematics in the past, and what are likely to be sources for future developments? Any serious answer to this question may influence examination of men's experience for new mathematical content as well as teaching for the future by stressing how the mathematics worked on by working mathematicians is shot through with the demands of time.

III. In the area of foreign languages, the science of education can effectuate a much needed change based on fact rather than belief:

1. What can one find from the apparent unsystematic learning of babies to improve the oversystematic approaches (grammatical, auditory, etc.) now in use in the teaching of foreign languages, approaches that only help a few while the first method of learning helps all?

2. What is the role of models in language learning? Many approaches to foreign language already answer that it is paramount. Does this or any other such common position stand close scrutiny?

3. Does a carefully built-up sequence of lessons starting with functioning, and accumulating vocabulary only later, reflect the natural sorting out of language more closely than does a logically rational approach from grammar or an approach based on a repetition of models?

4. Which is harder to learn, one's native language or a second language? (This study will require a new type of research in which a priori criticism of "the given" will supply the design of

experiments—which may reveal that consciousness plays the major part in learning.)

5. What are the differences between repetition and practice? How does the outcome of such a study affect the pedagogy of foreign languages?

6. Since words have no meaning of their own, meanings in a foreign language must be provided directly to the learners. Which techniques can do this while blocking the native language so that it does not interfere with the learning?

7. What makes one at ease with a new language?

8. Is there any reason to expect loss of memory of language if memory as such is not used in the learning of a language?

9. Is it unrealistic to conceive of teaching every child ten languages in ten years at school? Is the answer to this question fact or opinion? Can we forecast the effect on the child of learning a number of languages where at present he would learn only one?

10. Can it be proved that every human being can learn any language on earth?

11. Should students not be offered different ways of spending the time they use in learning languages, according to their aim in learning it (for a visit to a country, for business purposes, to become an interpreter, for translation purposes, etc.)?

12. Which exercises would permit every man to maintain flexible enough vocal organs so as to be able to have the vocal behaviors of a number of native groups?

IV. In the field of the natural and exact sciences, the science of education also has a contribution to make:

1. Which are the ways of knowing involved in each of the branches of physics, chemistry, biology? Are the branches of physics that are related to our senses—acoustics, optics, thermodynamics—different ways of knowing than electricity, astronomy, nuclear physics?

2. Are we aware through our senses unaided by any intervening element? Or is sensory awareness an elaboration of how we relate to the complex universe through our senses?

3. Is not science a study of qualities?

4. Is quantity a quality structuring other qualities?

5. Is it preferable in the study of science to begin with complex situations one learns to analyze or from principles that are acquired from previous researchers and exemplified in a priori models?

6. Is science education more a sharing of ways of knowing than a sharing of facts?

7. Is it true that the history of science is more than anything else a succession of corrections by the younger generation of what the older generation thought about the world? Are the facts of science what is left over from such discussions between successive generations?

8. What can we learn from the true great masters? What do we learn from the ordinary schools of research?

9. Is science education a proper study for all, irrespective of technological advances in one's culture and of laboratory conditions in schools? Or can science education go hand in hand only with technology?

10. Is technology, in relation to pure science, the sifting of what science learns is immediately meaningful in terms of everyday living? what is possible now? or what members of a culture find attractive to pursue?

11.   Fast-growing societies or nations have needs that demand more rather than less scientific education, in spite of their lack of technology, or perhaps because of it. Is it possible to develop an approach to natural sciences even on the minimal technology that exists in such societies and nations?

12.   Can science education be totally a growth in self-awareness in relation to the observable universe? What are instruments in terms of awareness?

13.   Is science education, education towards mastery of the environment? Is a study of the environment not a study of the awareness we have of it?

14.   Are scientists themselves the best science teachers? Or can we produce a group of people who understand the ways of knowing that is science and who can develop the techniques of making these ways available to learners?

V.   In the field of physical education the point of view of what is educable in us can provide a large group of investigations whose consequences may be welcome. Since what can be educated in us is our awareness, we must in this field come closer to our physical self—but a self conceived of as something animate rather than as just a system of articulated bones and muscles. Let us call "soma" what is usually referred to as "body" but this time include the individual will which is the component that moves the body.

1.   What changes in thinking result from the inclusion of the will in the explicit consideration of physical education?

2.   Can exercises of physical education affect the individual's will? Or is the absolute converse

the case, that without the participation of the will, there can be no progress of the physical basis?

3.   If the aim of physical education is deeper awareness of somatic functionings, which exercises are to be selected and which left out among those proposed all over the world and at all times for this purpose?

4.   Do games educate somatically or are they cultural devices to obtain from individuals adaptation to the overall needs of particular societies?

5.   Can we get some guidance for a "correct" physical education from the spontaneous education each child gives himself at various ages?

6.   Can we learn anything by closer study of animal behaviors? in particular, what it means to perfect behavior?

7.   Is there any functional reason for man's physical curve of growth? Why, for instance, is the rate of growth of the limbs not constant between birth and adulthood?

8.   Is there really any connection between various diets, various ways of life, and the mastery of the soma by individuals?

9.   Is it possible to associate with special exercises what one somatically needs to master before one manages performances similar to those of Olympic champions?

10   Can we make specialists in somatic mastery—and contribute to an analysis of the process so as to help improve physical education for all?

11.   Would it be part of somatic education to make students aware of all their somatic manifestations such as gait, breathing, chewing, yawning, etc.?

12. Is it true that the individual self comes to know his somatic expression better through certain non-somatic awarenesses he enters into, dwells in for some time, and transcends suddenly?

13. What impact on one's intellectual functions would a conscious somatic education have? Independence, autonomy, reliability, responsibility are overall attributes of the mind. Is their cultivation through somatic education either easier, or more lasting, or more easily transferable than through social or intellectual education?

14. Can somatic education become social education and education for love?

A general point in conclusion. Such studies (more could have been listed*) will attract different kinds of investigators who will develop different approaches and serve the science of education as researchers serve physics, by inventing methods of research dictated by the topic rather than b·· the total field. To the loss of all, this is not the case of so-called educational research at present, where the method seems independent of the topic.

The preceding section shows clearly that however new the education of awareness, the science of education, no one engaged in the research that is part of one's employment at college levels will find oneself without enough to do. Perhaps the list will help make plainer than it has been that trivial investigations are not likely to

---

* So as not to lengthen this section inordinately, we have passed over musical and artistic educations, both of which can benefit as much as all other educations from a study of what is educable in us. Some aspects of musical education have been touched upon in the practical chapter of the *Towards a Visual Culture*, mentioned earlier. In the field of social studies, many of the studies germane to a science of education are implicit in Chapter Three.

present themselves as solutions to complex educational challenges. Perhaps even other departments of universities will be inspired to conduct research as profound and broad as has been outlined above.

Indeed, everyone engaged in serious research is also engaged in education, since new findings demand of those who do not make them that they change their views or themselves so as to integrate the new in their vision of the world.

If the new is concerned with one's awareness, acceptance of significant scientific findings demands one's re-education. History is full of examples of social or institutional resistance to truth, to the ultimate disadvantage of society or the institution. Self-interest did not propose in these cases a solution that satisfied one's true interest. So institutional interest may be revealed later on as mere opinion and suicidal stubbornness.

Let us hope that modern men, who have been told of relativity for so many years, will recognize that their personal interest is to cooperate with what is affecting and changing the world. If it is true, as the result of over thirty years of work in this area has demonstrated to me, that the only education there can be is the education of awareness because awareness is what is educable in us, teachers of teachers will remain leaders in the field of education when they integrate this finding and bring themselves to work on what truly matters, some of which has been spelled out in the listings above.

Every few months or years a new science is born. This is only because one or more people have noted that they can study certain of their awarenesses, codify them, and call people's

attention to them. As soon as a sufficiently large
group of interested individuals has gathered around
these awarenesses, the value to society of the
science in question becomes apparent and the
public at large acknowledges the existence of an
established science with duties and prerogatives. A
journal, an association, prizes, conferences and
conventions, special chairs in institutions of higher
learning, all consolidate the special components of
the science.

In the case of the science of education, the
process will either be similar to this or, the
alternative that is clearly superior, it will be a
collective move of teachers of teachers from the
vocational activities offered at colleges today
towards a vast restructuring of college functions,
leading to serious responsible research and its
immediate translation into action in classrooms
everywhere.

Now, there is no doubt that only a vigorous
science already working smoothly and efficiently
could come up with such a list of important,
far-reaching, and immediately challenging topics of
research as have already been presented. Thus, it is
a matter of days only for a sufficient number of
teachers of teachers to be seriously at work to
glean results and impress the public that these
investigators understand what they are talking
about and can profoundly influence educational
practice.

Awareness unfortunately requires awareness to
be at work. This has been the brake upon the
emergence of educational scientists until today.

So long as instruction has remained the vehicle
of the trade, teachers of teachers have been
concerned at all levels with what, in effect, was

vocational education and dealt in recipes, comparing the efficacy of one against the other in achieving the desired result. Now that knowledge is running ahead of all, and knowing is the correct concept to use in the theory and practice of education, teachers of teachers no longer can waste time promoting habits that will become obstacles in the operations of their students. Teachers of teachers will continue to use the same time (that of their life, whether they teach as they did or in a new way), but more and more they necessarily will ask of themselves that its yield be adequate for the task they see at hand. From outside there may be no apparent change, at least in the beginning, because the whole change is an inner transformation. But these teachers of teachers, awareness of themselves having become one of their functionings, will at once see that this transformation is part of the fabric of life, of the laws of being human.

The obviousness of all this is reminiscent of what occurred during the Renaissance, when Europeans looked at the universe with new eyes and found so much to see and to report. Still, the Establishment burnt some of the seers, jailed others, exiled others, prevented some from making a living. Today we may be less ready to burn but as ready to ignore. Because we need to work first via self-interest, understood narrowly or otherwise, we have here to call teachers of teachers to a banquet and fireworks of important findings so as to secure the support rather than the opposition of the Establishment.

All this is neither crafty nor a compromise. It follows from a study of awareness of men's interests and how they set about taking care of these interests. I strongly hold that I shall not give myself to anything that does not promise me more than I am getting in terms of life and living from my present use of my time. This position I believe to be universal, and I have used it to increase the number of teachers who can give more and be less tired.

In this chapter I have addressed myself to teachers of teachers and invited them to take advantage of the existence of a science of education. If they do, I know from my work in the classroom that their students and the students of these students will benefit immeasurably by it.

Without the support of other teachers, all of us who are teachers of teachers are nothing. Hence, just as we can expect the teachers of teachers to join us for self-interest, they will have the classroom teachers on their side if they offer them what indeed looks to be their self-interest. In the classrooms this rule will apply and students will respond—that is to say, will be motivated—every time we can offer them evidence that their self-interest comes first in our teaching.

We have thus now reached a stage where all those who are involved in education can work together and benefit from each other's work. Because at this stage we can change time into experience at all levels, we can all experience fullness, joy, and meaningfulness, still recognizing that we need each other. The variety of experience does not make the unique process of changing time into experience less true or less the link between us all. Since science has made us much more tolerant than our good will could (because its process consists in finding how truth can be stated independently of the investigator and how to give to everyone the right of finding the truth and of showing it to others), a science of education, because it is a science, can use the same conditions of work to bring to all what has been found by one.

In the schools of the world a New Era is possible and it does not come from high ideals and from prophets—even though such influences can still apply—but because we have learned to work out the details of all the components belonging to the school situation. We are realists and full of hope. This very new state of affairs provides the tone of the New Era. The era of educational reform in the early twenties depended too much on lofty thoughts. Our era, in comparison, is rather pedestrian and open to all. We need everyone to bring it about.

To sum up. The task is immense, but it is manageable because we can be as many as there need to be, since all of us are invited to use our own gifts and to become aware of our own powers, which made their proofs at least in our babyhood.

The task, whose conceptualization is part of the functioning of a science (and of the technology that results from this science), does not represent the views of any one person but follows from the objectivation of what can be done with ourselves at the place, time, and stage where we find ourselves.

That the performing of this task is accompanied by a heightened level of joy is proof that its truth is not superficial. We become realists, capable of working as is required, but knowing throughout that this is a meaning of living: the exchange of time for experience.

Appendix
Notes on a New Epistemology:
Teaching and Education[*]

1.   Since no one to my knowledge has attempted
to base an epistemology on the powers of the mind
rather than on the impacts of the world upon the
mind, it may be of interest and value to provide an
example for discussion, leaving for a more
extensive writing the full discussion of the
approach and its applications. In this paper, the
focus of attention is related to number and
therefore has some bearing upon the teaching of
mathematics.

2.   The subtitle of these notes, "Teaching and
Education," is a natural by-product of the
discussion, for teaching has its basis in the
epistemology of its practitioners or in their beliefs
about how we know, and education is what is left
in the learner after his studies, and is concerned

* This paper was written for the fiftieth issue of *Mathematics Teaching*, the journal of the British Association of Teachers of Mathematics (ATM), founded by the author.

with the powers of the mind. In fact, a great deal of what is implied here is fundamental in my own studies of teaching and education over the last thirty years, and readers acquainted with my work may even find an echo of my Tuesday evening lectures given at London University twenty years ago. I say this to put into perspective some of the propositions that may have come to me at one or other of my recent seminars.

3.   For each of us, knowing is not an event that belongs to a particular date or a special occasion. It is synonymous rather with being conscious of one's functionings at any of the four levels of being: somatic, psychic, mental, spiritual.

We may use our observation and our insight to recapture our childhood's functionings, which is what I shall do in the notes that follow.

To learn to speak I must reach words and learn to control my utterances so that they correspond to what I will myself to utter, and in this process I can note among the sounds uttered by others those that a reader of this paper will make when he reads "two," "one," "four," "five," etc. I can retain these sounds as I retain others and utter them until I am satisfied that they sound like those I hear.

It is another awareness that will make me find that as words have an order in sentences, these sounds have an order in some of the utterances I hear. Hence I will embark on checking that I can utter them in the order accepted by my milieu, and so reach the mastery of the sequence

one, two, three, . . .

as far as I care to go. I may be two years old by now.

Since this sequence of sounds is part of me, no one has anything to say about what I should do with it. I may reverse the order and note that I can still produce a sequence. I may take a subset and practice a number of games in which only the sounds are involved and utter some and not utter others. All this is well within the powers of my mind; we know of examples of two or three year olds giving evidence that they are spontaneously interested in such sound games. For me, when I play such games, there is no need of anyone else, there is only the dialogue with myself and the content. The fact that I play such games reveals that an *order* structure, defined by *after* (or *before*), is available for this set of sounds, and that I know within myself whether this order is preserved or violated, just as anyone else can know, however old he is.*

4. Activities of the self are neither separated in watertight compartments nor dictated by the environment. Thus it is permissible for someone who walks to place his foot on the ground and simultaneously utter one of the sequences of sounds so as to produce a one-to-one correspondence between two time sequences involving oneself.

In my own awareness the activities now merge, and I shall be able to use the new one if I transfer my power, my energy, from my foot to my hand or to my neck or to my eyes or from any one of these to anything else that is just as much a part of

---

* There is nothing remarkable in this. We note that the order of grammatical functions in sentences used by the environment is much more complex than the linear one referred to above and that no one challenges that small children sometimes reach fluency of speech only a little after their first birthday.

myself. These coordinations of sequences of gestures and utterances I shall call *counting*. This is now seen as my own doing, and is not at all a matter of any teaching I have received. Indeed, I do not need to be taught and, like the supposed inventor of counting, I find in myself by myself the co-existence of these two sequences, which I control by matching so as to give myself the power of using them simultaneously.

While I am engaged in doing this I have no concern to please anyone, but only to succeed in achieving what I see is achievable in my own system.

5.   Soon, among several other questions, I shall hear in the environment the question "how many?" and find that it is being answered precisely by the new synthesis available to me called counting. Hence we see that counting is the answer to "how many?" and only needs the mastery of two easily performed activities—utterance of a sequence of sounds while a part of one's soma moves rhythmically over the discrete elements of the set concerned. Let us call *numeral* the awareness that the sounds learned earlier and put into sequence serve to answer the question "how many?".

Numerals are therefore felt in the self not as an attribute of the situation per se, but as the demand it makes on us to know it from the angle of this special mobilization of our throat and some other parts of our soma.

6.   Soon I perceive that I can save energy when I count by moving my soma economically, and delegate to my ocular muscle the movements I

performed either with my hand or my neck. This transmission, from hand or neck to ocular muscle, can then be made swifter so as to give the impression to myself that I take in the numeral at once, when in fact it is only a speeded-up use of part of myself similar to the speeding-up I already have achieved in the various skills (walking, speaking, . . .) I have learned. Hence because I can take in quickly the numeral of a given set of objects, I believe it to be an attribute of the situation I am looking at. In fact, if I give myself a more numerous set, this belief vanishes and I need to resort again to the clumsy approach I used at the beginning. True, I can educate myself and widen the set I can handle swiftly, as virtuosos do, but I may prefer not to.

A numeral, although, like color, grammatically an adjective, mobilizes me differently from a color, which can be known at once by me because of its physico-chemical impact on my soma. The perception of a numeral has needed the education of my whole self, the coordination of the inner dynamics of my mind taking in simultaneously a variety of functionings.

7. Hence I can return to the structures of my mind (which are equivalent to this arsenal) called the sequence of numerals and to my experience of counting, and discover in the structures much that is new to me and perhaps to others. For instance, I am ready to notice that the counting sequence used by my environment (and that I shall learn one day has been handed down historically) presents interesting auditory features, such as regularities: *four* gives *forty*, *six* gives *sixty*, etc. I can also notice that, as in the language I have learned,

savings occur because of combinations, repetitions, and the use of a small number of building units. So I can note quite early that if I say

one, two, three, . . . nine,

except for the sequence

ten, eleven, twelve, . . . nineteen,

the following sequences require only that I notice a pattern, and I begin to practice:

twenty, twenty-one, . . . twenty-nine,
thirty, thirty-one, . . . thirty-nine, . . .

I discover that I need, indeed, only a small number of sounds and a small number of principles in order to be as good as my elders in uttering the first ninety-nine numerals.

This I do independently of answering the question "how many?", but accomplish merely in order to master the other meanings of counting, the uttering of the sequence of numerals as developed historically.*

8. When the numeral "one hundred" appears, just one new sound will permit me to reach nine hundred and ninety-nine, and I show that the power of reaching so far fascinates me by entering spontaneously the job of uttering this sequence at the slightest provocation, as many times as is needed, until I know all I need to know at this stage. I shall count while going to the park and coming home in order to know whether it takes as long to go as to come back, between street lights or between traffic lights, before I sleep, or until my food may be swallowed.

---

* It is unfortunate that educators have not produced two words for such different activities. Perhaps the semantic unclarity indicates a confusion of thinking.

I now have a reliable frame of reference; an inner clock; a mastered sequence with which I am familiar, that I have made myself, consciously, more or less laboriously, that I know to be mine and to which I shall soon refer in so many different ways.

For indeed it has features I can work on.

9.   For instance, although I can vary the time taken to move from one utterance to the next, although the uttering of the numerals takes longer as I move on in the sequence, I can see to it that the time separating two successive utterances is constant and feel it to be so. This temporal constant will act as a strong structurer of the sequence, giving it the character of an arithmetic progression (in the technical sense of the word), and thereby generating the constancy of the unit, even though the act of doing so is not a consequence of any or all of the demands of my past experience. Indeed I may have counted a set of fruit consisting of a plum, a banana, a peach, an apple, and a pear, knowing that all are different, non-comparable, but ending up certain that there were five pieces of fruit there.

It is therefore in myself, in the cadence of my gestures, and not in the temporal sequence affecting my sensibility, that I find the sense that a unit exists behind the sequence of non-comparable sounds considered as sounds.

10.   I can play another game of matching if it is proposed to me.

I already know a lot about classes and isomorphism simply from looking at the world around me where nothing is ever seen under the same light, from the same distance, or at the same angle. For I recognize everything in spite of the multitude of transformations affecting it.

So if I am shown the arabic numerals as a system of signs that display the properties of the sounds I know, it will take only such time as I need to be sure of how each sign triggers the particular corresponding sound to master the new system as an isomorphism of the one I already own. The properties I know are not yet mathematical; they are only the ones mentioned above. So I can learn to utter at the rhythm of a pointer any one of the nine hundred ninety-nine subsets we can form from one, two, or three of the following signs, starting at the bottom line and moving upwards in a constant time sequence.*

1	2	3	4	5	6	7	8	9
10	20	30	40	50	60	70	80	90
100	200	300	400	500	600	700	800	900

In fact the table has many advantages (which I have mentioned elsewhere**) and can be used systematically to place five or six year olds in front of the full extension of the operations on the whole numbers in any base of numeration. This I shall not describe here, although I have given

---

* We can count exactly the "burden to the memory" represented by what actually needs to be remembered for the full sequence to be generated. On the first line, "one," "two," "three," "four," "five," "six," "seven," "eight," "nine," or *nine* signs; on the second line, "ten," "twenty," "thirty," "fifty," "-ty," of *five* signs, plus "eleven," "twelve," "thirteen," "fifteen," "-teen," or another *five*; and on the third line, "a hundred"—or *twenty* sign-sound combinations altogether. The fact that we can make this calculation I feel, is another element that shows that we are on a good track in this new epistemology, for it allows us to estimate exactly the role of the environment and the role of the mind.

** Book 2 of *Mathematics with Numbers in Colour*, Educational Explorers, 1961; and *Mathematics Teaching*, no 39.

lessons to a number of classes to indicate its feasibility.

11. Up to now we have recognized as the elements of our numerical experience:

— the sounds of the numerals being like any other sounds in our speech,

— the possibility of these sounds forming a sequence,

— the use of this sequence in counting as the answer to "how many?",

— the use of this sequence in a number of games played by the individual child, in particular the one that generates the feeling that the time separating successive utterances may be made constant,

— the provision of an isomorphic set of visual triggers that will give a system of signs representing the system of sounds already owned by the child, and displaying many of its properties.

It is clear that whenever a set is given where counting gives the numeral we do not have to *produce* the set that has been given to us. But on occasions we may be asked to produce a set from elements of a set about which we do not need to know much. For instance, we can be asked to produce six glasses of beer from a cask. Six is here a numeral when the operation is over, but it is an *operator* while the drawing is taking place. This distinction may be subtle, but it nevertheless exists and is easily acknowledged when we consider that in asking for three pounds of pears or two bags of potatoes there is the need for a special action to generate the result. This action is reminiscent of the ordinal quality of counting *on* one's fingers rather than the counting *of* one's fingers. We must, in effect, arrive at the numeral, not show how many objects there are. (In this respect the question, "Show me five with a finger," would have a meaning, the answer to which would be to show one finger, the one labeled five in the counting.) Hence we can add to the list above the recognition that number can be an operator, although it is still not yet a mathematical entity.

12.   The fact that we can play a variety of games with these systems of signs and sounds merely because they exist in the mind and because our mind is endowed with its own dynamics, puts to us the question of when we shall need to come to the awareness of numbers as mathematicians know them.

It is important to distinguish the use of "numbers" as mathematicians do it. Sometimes numbers are only elements of the sequence of numerals, as when suffixes or exponents are being used. Sometimes numbers are entities that have been endowed through some operation or operations with the possibility of owning or not owning some property (e.g., prime numbers). I shall call *numbers* only the latter, that is, there will be no awareness of "numberness" unless there is simultaneously an awareness of one or more algebras permitting the creation of classes of equivalences for the entity so that depending on the problem involving the entity it can be known which equivalent form corresponds to this problem.

Until this section we have not been concerned with numbers. We can do a great deal that teachers believe to be arithmetic but which really only involves numerals, the dynamics of the mind being there in any case. Because of these dynamics, we can get the illusion that we are doing mathematics when in fact numbers as defined above do not appear at all.

For instance: in the sequence one, two, three, etc., if we utter the first, skip the second, utter the next, and so on, we form two sub-sequences—

one, three, five, . . . , eleven, thirteen, . . . , twenty-one, . . .

and—

two, four, six, . . . , twelve, fourteen, . . . , twenty-two, . . .

These sequences we may christen the *odd* and *even* numerals and we can write them in arabic signs:

$$1, 3, 5, \ldots, 11, 13, \ldots, 21, 23, \ldots$$
$$2, 4, 6, \ldots, 12, 14, \ldots, 22, 24, \ldots$$

and state: *numerals whose signs end in 1, 3, 5, 7, 9, are odd, and those ending in 0, 2, 4, 6, 8 are even*—without having said anything requiring numbers.

We can do much more, as anyone thinking in this direction will find.

It is even possible to generate algebras on numerals, which show how far we can go without the assumption that a unit is required to build the sequence of numerals. This will be illuminating to anyone who studied analysis after Peano and Landau.

13.   So far I have avoided even the use of words such as *cardinal* and *ordinal*, and indeed I can see that the currently accepted epistemology has not noticed that what is called "cardinal" is the awareness that the numeral is to be found in the self and not in the set, and that the definition of a

cardinal is equivalent to saying that numerals as words share the property of words, that is, they apply to all situations that are defined at the same time as some transformations that keep some property stressed, while all others are ignored. In other words, "five is a word" is as good a definition as "five is the cardinal of all sets equivalent to one called five."

To give a numeral a new property, which we can call its *cardinality*, we need to think simultaneously of its ordinality, so that when I look at a set and know its numeral, I relate this numeral to its predecessors and its immediate followers. Then I can see that cardinality is new and has a future, for I do not stop at this set and the feeling that I moved my head such-and-such number of times to scan it, but I find that I could have stopped before and given the numeral of all its subsets since I am free to count as I wish.

Hence cardinality is pregnant with the possibility of comparing the subsets in the set and hence with the algebras; this will generate numbers.

In particular, the cardinal of a set is defined by the awareness that the numeral we associate with it will occur whatever way we count the set. This invariance with respect to counting creates a class of equivalence for the set, and it is this that has a future because now we have more awareness than before that we can do what was not required by counting. In this lies the shift from some activities of the self to an awareness of mathematics as a sui generis activity of the mind, an activity that again chooses to stress some aspect of the relationships involved while ignoring others.

To this one can return later and open up the question again.

14. To sum up this short preliminary discussion of a new proposal for the foundation of mathematics, it seems clear that if we start with the innocent mind and move towards the awareness of what is sui generis in mathematics, we cannot escape the fact that we are dealing with a substance as subtle as that which we met in speech at the beginning of life, and that awareness of what can be done with this provides a great deal that has been left unused so far. We can therefore hope for new findings in epistemology if we use as our starting point powers of the mind instead of memories and go on to improve our education of the coming generation by being allies of their functionings rather than followers of the justification by some adult of what he thinks.

Bibliographical Note

Among the sixty books written by the author, the following titles can serve readers who wish to delve further into his work.

PSYCHOLOGY

Introduction à la Psychologie de L'Affectivité (Neuchâtel, France: Delachaux et Niestlé, 1952). This work has been translated into English, Portuguese, and Spanish.

Un Nouveau Phénomène Psychosomatique (Neuchâtel, France: Delachaux et Niestlé, 1952).

Conscience de la Conscience (Neuchâtel, France: Delachaux et Niestlé, 1967).

TEACHING OF MATHEMATICS

Teaching Mathematics to Deaf Children (Reading, England: Educational Explorers, 1958).

For the Teaching of Mathematics, Vol. I–III (Reading, England: Educational Explorers, 1962-63). These volumes have been translated into French, Italian, and Spanish.

117

TEACHING FOREIGN LANGUAGES

Teaching Foreign Languages in Schools (Reading, England: Educational Explorers, 1963).

The Silent Way in Spanish/French/English (Reading, England: Educational Explorers, 1964-66).

MISCELLANEOUS

The White Canary (Reading, England: Educational Explorers, 1968). A story for children.

Towards A Visual Culture (New York: Outerbridge & Dienstfrey, 1969).

Dr. Gattegno is also the publisher of *My Life and My Work Series* (Reading, England: Educational Explorers) which contains thirty titles, each by a different author, with an equal number now in preparation.

Information about these books is available from Educational Solutions, Inc., Box 190 Cooper Station, New York City, New York 10003

118